THE COLLECTED POEMS
OF ÉDOUARD GLISSANT

THE COLLECTED POEMS
OF ÉDOUARD GLISSANT

ÉDOUARD GLISSANT

Edited and with an Introduction by Jeff Humphries

Translated by Jeff Humphries with Melissa Manolas

UNIVERSITY OF MINNESOTA PRESS

MINNEAPOLIS • LONDON

The University of Minnesota Press gratefully acknowledges financial assistance provided by the French Ministry of Culture for the translation of this book and by the Louisiana State University Foundation for its production.

The translators gratefully acknowledge the award of a fellowship by the National Endowment for the Humanities to support the work on this volume.

Originally published as *Poèmes complets* by Édouard Glissant. Copyright 1994 Éditions Gallimard

Riveted Blood, Black Salt, and *Yokes* were first published in English, translated by Betsy Wing, in *Black Salt: Poems* by Édouard Glissant. Copyright 1998 University of Michigan Press. New translations of these poems appear in this book.

Published by the University of Minnesota Press
111 Third Avenue South, Suite 290
Minneapolis, MN 55401-2520
http://www.upress.umn.edu

Library of Congress Cataloging-in-Publication Data

Glissant, Édouard, 1928–
[Poems. English]
The collected poems of Édouard Glissant / Édouard Glissant ;
translated by Jeff Humphries with Melissa Manolas ; edited and with an
introduction by Jeff Humphries.
p. cm.
ISBN 978-0-8166-4195-6 (pb)
I. Humphries, Jefferson, 1955– II. Manolas, Melissa. III. Title.
PQ3949.2.G53A24 2005
841'.914—dc22
2004029228

Printed in the United States of America on acid-free paper

The University of Minnesota is an equal-opportunity educator and employer.

24 22 23 22 21 20 19   10 9 8 7 6 5 4 3 2 1

CONTENTS

Introduction JEFF HUMPHRIES xi

THE COLLECTED POEMS OF ÉDOUARD GLISSANT

RIVETED BLOOD
  Eyes Voice 6
  November 7
  Savage Reading 8
  Rock 9
  Slow Train 10
  Tree Great Tree 11
  Black Smoke 12
  Elements 13
  Nourishing Air 17
  Cities 19
  Confession 20
  Vertigo in Cold Weather 22
  Glory 23
  To Die, Not to Die 24

Temptations   25

Solitude   26

Beauty   27

Abrupt   28

Mainstay   29

The Dead and Living Tree   30

A FIELD OF ISLANDS   33

THE RESTLESS EARTH

Theater   49

Ocean   50

Incantation   51

Morning   52

The Bay of the Sky   53

Secret Cliff   54

Promenade of Solitary Death   57

The Book of Offerings   59

The House of Sands   61

Verses   63

Consecration   66

THE INDIES   69

BLACK SALT

The First Day   103

Carthage   108

Salt Taxes   114

Africa   118

Wounds   123

High Noon   128

Acclamation   132

YOKES

Gorée   135

Burned Field   136

Fats   137

House for the Dead   138

Behanzin   139

Country   140

Iron-dogs   141

Letters of Calling   142

Country   143

In Savane Square   144

Privileged Prose   145

Factory Still   146

Country   147

Moreover   148

Prose   149

Dlan   150

Dlan   151

Dlan   152

The Doubter   153

The Doubter   154

Trace   155

Role   156

Ashes   157

Language   158

Country   159

Deafer Than the Sea   160

Salt Marshes   161

Country   162

Pretty Men   163

Green Ray   164

Vaval   165

Mangroves   166

Poetic   167

Cactus   168

In Actuality   169

Study Days   170

The Alchemist's Fire   171

Fiefs   172

Ideal   173

Ball and Chain or Ash   174

Strike   175

"Within the Budding Pineapple Groves"   176

Guadeloupe   177

Ones   178

Throttle   179

Tomorrows   180

DREAM COUNTRY, REAL COUNTRY

Country   183

The Country of Before   185

Ata-Eli, the Blind Man, and Ichneumon   188

Song of Ichneumon   190

For Laoka   191

Song of Thael and Matthew   193

For Mycea   196

Country   199

Traces   201

FASTES   205

THE GREAT CHAOSES
    Bayou   225
    The Great Chaoses   231
    The Stolen Eye   239
    Wooded Regions   246
    The Volcano's Water   250

INTRODUCTION

JEFF HUMPHRIES

Author of nine volumes of poetry, seven books of essays and literary criticism, and eight novels, Édouard Glissant is widely acknowledged as one of the two or three most important Caribbean writers of the past half century and one of the most significant writers presently working in French. His potential importance for postcolonial studies has only just begun to be recognized, thanks to the excellent work of Michael Dash, the most knowledgeable and reliable scholar of Glissant's work, and, more recently, that of Celia Britton. Recipient of the Prix Renaudot in fiction for *La Lézarde* (1958) and the Prix Charles Veillon for his novel *Le Quatrième Siècle,* as well as several times a finalist for the Nobel Prize in Literature, in 1991 Glissant was awarded the inaugural Grand Prix Roger Caillois by the city of Reims for his entire body of work. Jean-Louis Joubert has said that his "clear-sightedness and breadth of thought, [his] innovativeness of literary structure place Glissant in the forefront of late-twentieth-century literary production." According to Gilles Anquetil, writing in *Le Nouvel Observateur,* "he is without doubt our most beautiful writer in the French language today," and his writing is "sumptuous and proliferous, . . . a whirlwind of the imaginary." The *Journal* of Geneva has declared him "a colossus: . . . his work has made the Antillean voice the most respected and listened to [in French]."[1]

The theoretical underpinnings of Glissant's literary works are nowhere more accessible or more vivid than in his poems, and these constitute a resource for postcolonial studies of inestimable value for several reasons.

First, Glissant's work owes considerably less to European (colonizing) theorists (Karl Marx, Jacques Derrida, Michel Foucault, Jacques Lacan) than does that of Homi Bhabha, Gayatri Spivak, or Edward Said. Glissant's work is instead grounded in specifically Caribbean history, geography, nature, and language. It can stand on its own without the theoretical basis of European philosophy, relying instead on the peculiar but universal relations between man and nature, human languages and those of wind, sun, trees, vines, flowers, fish, and birds in the strange resplendently tragic and exotic place called the Antilles—a place that Columbus first took to be Japan (the gateway to Asia) and which then was shaped by European violence (the virtual extirpation of the native peoples, who still survive only in a state of mixture, *creolization,* with European and African blood) and imagination, first into a plantation-based economy dependent on slavery and today into a place shaped by European notions of the exotic into a tourist commodity. No region of the world so directly shows the imprint of white European imagination (imposed violently and nonviolently), and no other so vividly displays the recourses and the consequences of displacement, enslavement, resistance, and miscegenation. The work of Patrick Chamoiseau, Raphaël Confiant, Daniel Maximin, and an entire younger generation of literary thinkers of "Antillianity" is based on the writing of Glissant, because Glissant's work is grounded in the Antilles, not in European theory.

The advantages of Glissant's thought probably have something to do with its being less well known than that of some other postcolonial thinkers who owe more to European theories: we have already embraced the European theorists and are reassured by familiar references to them. Glissant's work is less contained by the discourses of intellectual colonization because it is less *reactionary* than that of Said, Bhabha, or Spivak, and more positive without being in the least naive or limited in scope. It is potentially far more liberating to far more people because it is not first or only a reaction to European theories, and, while growing out of the specificities of the Caribbean, it is grounded in the universal aspects of that region. In many respects, no region of the world is more exemplary of the world in its present state than this.

Glissant's ideas of Antillianity, Caribbeanness, and *métissage* (miscegenation or intermingling) describe processes that involve much richer and greater possibilities of personal and national growth and freedom that extend beyond the known limitations of European theories, reaching into the future instead of back to a past that we know already and perhaps are more comfortable with in spite of its acknowledged restrictions.

Born in Martinique in 1928, Édouard Glissant attended the Lycée Victor Schoelcher in Fort-de-France, where Aimé Césaire taught and Frantz Fanon (two years older than Glissant) was also a student. Here Glissant was exposed early on to Césaire's poetical ideology of negritude, which he never embraced and would soon reject outright for both literary and political reasons (in Martinique even more than in France, the political and the literary have never pretended to be separate). Here he was also introduced to French literary modernism, which in the person of André Breton (who visited Martinique in 1941) had had a profound influence on Césaire. Later, in Paris, Glissant studied philosophy at the Sorbonne, where he took a *licence* and eventually a *doctorat d'etat* and ethnology at the Musée de l'Homme. Among Caribbean writers, Glissant's thought is unique for its rejection of any simple or static concept of the relation between literature and politics, poetry and ideology.

LITERARY ANTECEDENTS

Stéphane Mallarmé

It is impossible to read Glissant's poetry or prose without being aware of the influence of Stéphane Mallarmé. Mallarmé's presence is felt above all in Glissant's sense and use of the French language, the sheer virtuosity and difficulty as well as the musicality of his writing. But Glissant combines neologisms, anachronistic syntax, and vocabulary—all recognizable symbolist practices—with the use of Creole words and expressions, which signify a rejection of the metropolitan, colonizing language's claims to a totalized purity of expression. Mallarmé saw in poetry a means of achieving an aesthetic purity that was impossible in the real world ("I say: flower! . . . and there arises . . . that one which is absent from every bouquet"),[2] of creating an "artificial reality" defined by a relation of negativity and absence with respect to the world of mundane experience. For the true Mallarmean adherent and practitioner of poetry, the everyday must be supplanted, rendered moot by the pure, empty hermetic forms of poetic language. This ultimate expression of late-nineteenth-century idealism/symbolism had its roots in Baudelaire's and Theophile Gautier's "Parnassian" preference for artificial realities, and the former's horror of nature and its apparently chaotic "prolixities," which only poetic artifice could redeem.

Glissant embraces the hermeticism of Mallarmé while rejecting the latter's view of nature as a corrupting and antipoetical force. In *L'Intention poétique*, Glissant wrote that "the work of a poet seems (to this poet) ridiculous by comparison with what he dreamed: it is never more than the foam of the ocean from which he wishes to wrest a cathedral, a definitive architecture. Mallarmé is one of those rare individuals who have acknowledged this lack, cultivated this absence; to the point of making absence into a presence, and in a way turning the weakness of poetry into its goal."[3] This passage reveals a mixture of admiration for Mallarmé's poetic accomplishment and rejection of its pretensions.

Instead of replacing or supplanting anything real, poetry becomes for Glissant an expression and extension of nature, which without any literary intervention is at least as inscrutable and beautiful as a poem. (It is not accidental that one of his novels, *La Lézarde*, should be named for a river, and another, *Mahogany*, for a tree.) In this sense, Glissant's poetic language, while resembling that of Mallarmé superficially, is more like that of traditional Chinese and Japanese poetry, in which there is no concept of nature in the Western sense—as defined by its difference from the human world of artifice—and no sense of human experience or aesthetic production as distinct from "nature": instead, writing is understood as "unfurling" from the natural just as a flower opens.

Arthur Rimbaud

This poetics of "unfurling," as well as Arthur Rimbaud's shared artistic vision, characterized by exile and literal, ongoing displacement, makes Glissant closer to him in poetic practice and vision than to Mallarmé or any other nineteenth-century poet. Rimbaud pursued another idea implicit in the vision of Baudelaire: that poetry could and should be the means of entering into communion with the hidden essences, the occulted purity of Nature. For Glissant, this purity is not assumed to be occulted or vitiated prior to poetic experience; there is no need for a poetical "transmutation" or transcendence of Nature, which is seen as already expressing the essence of poetry in its purest state: the opacity and interrelatedness of signs, the perpetual flux of meaning and experience, the nonintegrity of the perceiving subject. The ongoing mutual "contamination" of natural phenomena and the "impurity" and flux of lived experience are not for Glissant things to be redeemed by a gnostic and hermetic aestheticism; they rather define the very essence of the literary.

Rimbaud's pronounced sense of the poet as displaced, and of poetic subjectivity as indistinguishable from the experience of temporal and spatial displacement (exile), is also very much closer to Glissant than anything in Mallarmé or Baudelaire. While Mallarmé went beyond Baudelaire in embracing the idea of the poetic subject as a phenomenon effectively "abolished" by and in the act of writing ("the elocutionary disappearance of the poet, who cedes the initiative to words"), this aspect of his thought is contradicted by the concept of the poet as a kind of gnostic sage-redeemer, whose achievement is to construct an alternative world characterized by a purity that does not exist in nature or lived experience. Much the same contradiction runs throughout the work of Baudelaire, though its expression is less explicit and highly developed. In this sense both Baudelaire and Mallarmé cling to the idea of the Master Subject Who Knows *(le sujet supposé savoir)*, conceiving the poet as the agent, the "maker" of poetry; Rimbaud goes beyond both in conceiving genuine poetic experience as beginning only when subjectivity breaks down ("Il faut se faire voyant . . ."). Because of his acculturation and identification with the traditions of Western thought, Rimbaud held that poetic consciousness could come about only through a violent assault by the poet on her or his own constituted self, through excess, hallucination, and depravity. On this point, there is a fundamental difference from Glissant, who does not see his own poetic consciousness as defined or restricted by any Western traditions of totalization and artifice. The poet of the New World, whether of European, African, or mixed ancestry, is already displaced, exiled, errant at birth, and has no need of self-destructive behavior in order to realize an intimacy with Nature or to achieve a poetic vision of the pure essences in Nature, because, even when betrayed from within by identification with Old World Western ways of knowing, he or she already lives and knows in a relation of nondistinction from the natural, the real, and history, and enjoys a fundamental intimacy with natural experience that has only to be recognized and cultivated to become explicit. In Rimbaud's poetic journey of displacement, this kind of conciliation with Essence, with Nature, can come about only by rupturing the intricately woven structures of the self *(le sujet supposé savoir)* through violent self-abasement.

By contrast with the harsh, nightmarish landscape of Rimbaud's "Bateau ivre," Glissant's New World is a lush, hallucinatory land of displacement *and* reconciliation, an earthy embodiment both of postmodern humanity's alienation from nature and of the possibility of a return to it, deeply scarred by the incursions, intellectual and political, of European civilization and yet exempted from its limitations of thought and experience. This is a place where *métissage* (mongrelization) is palpable everywhere, in which beauty is always *impure,* arising out of the prolixity of intermingled cultures, races, and languages. While the scene and object of all his work are literally the Caribbean Islands, these become palpable figures for all of human experience, a place and time of expatriation, genocide, and also a sultry beauty, unique to the islands, where women and men live and think with the forces of nature, not against them. These lines from *The Indies* exemplify Glissant's vision of the violent European intervention that began the present era of Caribbean modernity:

> *1492. The Great Discoverers hurl themselves upon the Atlantic, in search of the Indies. With them begins the poem. Also all those, before and after this New Day, who have known their dream, lived off it or died from it. . . .*
>
> *These conquerors lusted to death after the gold and silver mines of the New World. They vanquished the banks, then the forest, then the Andes, then the High Plains with their deserted cities. They sacked the very space, in their covetous and insanely mystical fury. Tragic Song of love for the New World. Progressive exaltation, massacre, and final solitude. A rupture is consummated; but man does not give up the dream. He will repopulate what he has depopulated. Pillage shall be followed by pillage. The various names of the Conqueror: Cortez, Pizarro, Almagro, Balboa. The insane assassin: Father Valverde. The one he baptized before strangling: Atahualpa, last lover of the red earth.*

In this context, the discovery of the New World, with the slave trade, the European war on Native American societies, and the rape and pillage of the land to make room for agriculture and industry, marks the beginning of our present, uneasy consciousness, our sense of a loss that we cannot ever define very satisfactorily or precisely, and yet which defines for us the possibilities of beauty as well as of daily subsistence and political progress. Glissant's advice, politically and poetically, is that we must embrace the multiplicitousness, the *disorder* of Nature (an abomination to Mallarmé and Baudelaire), which within the human sphere is none other than *métissage,* nonintegrity. Only through doing so does there lie any hope of superseding the violence of the past or the loss and displacement of the present. In these three stanzas from *The Restless Earth,* there is the promise of such hope, but, as so often in Glissant's poetry, also a sense of loss, of perpetual mourning and deferred hope:

> Silence had fled the ardent solitude
> Triumphal Palms! The deserted day swept upon the flowers;
> Ever in between fear and desire, hesitates
> The wounded love that shall strew the day.
>
> O night, country of carnage of opprobrium,
> Of larvae that endlessly foretell their future
> To the skies where sleeps the sempiternal bird.

Glissant's poetry, while closer to Rimbaud in many respects than to Mallarmé, never approaches the affinity recognized by many critics between Césaire and Rimbaud. This difference with respect to Rimbaud is not just a matter of style; it also reflects Glissant's rejection of the overtly ideological poetics of Leopold Senghor's—not Césaire's—negritude. Senghor's vision, with which Césaire is often misleadingly associated, is grounded in an ideological nostalgia for the African origins of Caribbean culture *(negritude)* and parallels Rimbaud's quest for a totalizing poetic vision (the ultimate project of symbolism). It might be said that the violence of Rimbaud's language and vision corresponds more nearly to the explosive rhetoric of Césaire's poetry than to anything in Glissant, who characterized the affinity between Césaire and Rimbaud in terms of a poetics of *fulguration;* but in fact that same rhetorical and thematic violence is just barely sublimated in Glissant's poetry, infusing the language with an intense, if subterranean, heat.

André Breton

The great surrealist André Breton had championed the work of Césaire, and he came to Martinique in 1941, while Glissant was a student. The impact of Breton and surrealism is evident in Glissant's style, as in his tendencies to catachresis (extreme metaphor) and to juxtaposing images or combining adjectives and nouns, nouns and verbs that logically cannot go together. This tendency becomes more pronounced in Glissant's poetry since 1980; the language of surrealism is especially well suited to represent what Glissant calls "the Chaos World," a world in which meaning arises *virtually,* as relation, from the interstices of discordant images and words. But it must be remembered that Glissant deploys these means to an end very different from that of Breton and the surrealists; he is not a literary anarchist who believes in disorder for its own sake. Rather, in Glissant's work, apparent chaos is the source of all meaning and order, and is both natural and meaningful.

Aimé Césaire and Saint-John Perse (Alexis Leger)

Of all twentieth-century French poets, the one Glissant claims as closest to his vision and voice is Saint-John Perse, whom Glissant has said to be "often present in the clearing of my words"[4] and in whose work Glissant claims to have discovered an alternative to the fulguration of Césaire's negritude: the poetics of *accumulation:* "Fulguration is the art of blocking obscurity in its revealed light; accumulation, that of consecrating the obvious upon its duration, at last perceived. Fulguration is a function of self, accumulation a matter of community."[5] In graphic terms, the fulgurative poetics of Rimbaud and Césaire strives for a blast, a vertical instant of ascesis, while the accumulative mode of Glissant and Perse conceives poetic truth as dispersed, enduring, an unpredictable horizontal line that may shift gently or abruptly up or down in its level of intensity but is always deferred, unfurling into the future, never fully present in any one place or time. In Glissant's view, this is how it is supposed to work. But the specific opposition of Césaire's style to Perse's leads us to wonder if in fact Glissant's embrace of Perse as an influence is not a means of obscuring the influence of Césaire. As the first French Caribbean literary figure to be accepted and celebrated in Europe, and a teacher at the school he attended, Césaire's influence on Glissant could not be avoided, however much the latter may deny it. Fulguration must be only the "vertical" expression of the very thing that accumulation delivers in a "horizontal" format. It is my opinion that we cannot consider the influence of Perse on Glissant without acknowledging that this is very probably a covering figure for the influence of Césaire, whose writings were deeply inflected by the very European antecedents already acknowledged as influences on Glissant's work—Mallarmé, Rimbaud, Breton.

Césaire's concept of negritude is usually misunderstood as being grounded in a sense of nostalgia for African origins and a sort of pan-African essentialism; this is true of Senghor's negritude but not of Césaire's. Césaire has underscored this defining difference, saying that as an African, Senghor's experience was vastly different from Césaire's Caribbean one. Césaire's negritude is only metaphorically racial. Everyone who is in any sense exiled, displaced, disenfranchised in the world, everyone whose sense of identity is grounded in miscegenation—literal or figural—is *negre,* in Césaire's view. This brings the reliance of Glissant's concepts of *métissage* and Antillianity on Césaire's negritude into clear focus. Césaire's negritude, though not Senghor's, can be said to have anticipated Glissant's theories of Caribbeanness because it rejects racial essentialism.

While without African ancestry, Perse was of Caribbean origin, from Guadeloupe; a diplomat and foreign ministry official, his opposition to the German occupation during World War II forced him into exile in anglophone North America. There is a division in Perse's poetic vision between the European and the Caribbean, ancestry and origin. The "warm porosity," "liquid space," and "multilayered opacity" of Perse's early work represent for Glissant his authentically Caribbean aspect,[6] and a safely distant, different poetic influence by contrast with that of Césaire, which is so close, so much the same that it might "cover" and extinguish Glissant's own emerging poetic identity, according to the paradigm of influence elucidated by Harold Bloom. Perse's later work is dominated by a more European desire to totalize the world in the static and artificial forms of an abstract poetry. By contrast with the traditional strictures of European poetry that correspond to its temperate and cultivated landscape, Glissant saw in Perse's Caribbean side the exemplar of a neotropical style: "Perse is Caribbean," he wrote, "in the tangled, primitive growth of his style." In Perse's early poetry, as in Glissant's, "nature speaks first within us." Through Perse, Glissant comes to embrace the oriental notion of writing as unfurling from nature, not opposing or containing its excess but arising out of it: "[Perse's] nature is the word as vegetation."[7]

Michael J. Dash has identified four aspects of Perse's early poetry that influenced Glissant: the polyphony of Perse's poetic voice and his use of multiple personae within a single text; his view of the text as an essentially natural, therefore precarious and mutable, phenomenon, "built upon nothing," subject to the vagaries of other natural forces such as wind and rain, like marks ("Seamarks," the English title of one of Perse's books of poetry) made in the sand of a beach (in stark contrast with the symbolist ideal of the poem as monument); the image of the sea as emblem of both knowledge *(accumulation)* and displacement *(errance),* interrelatedness *(relation)* and impurity *(métissage),* its fluidity and shifting tides the natural model for a poetry and a poetic subjectivity whose relation to the world is always shifting and evolving, never fixed, in which the simple binarisms of ideological literature are dissolved by the corrosive effects of elemental flux; and finally, the use of the prose poem as the form most suited to a poetics of duration and accumulation.[8] Underlying all these is the view of nature not as the analogue of poetry but its very source and substance, a grounding motif of Perse's early work, which is contradicted by the affectations of his later, less Caribbean poems. There is not one of these aspects that cannot also be attributed to Césaire.

William Faulkner

Glissant has repeatedly acknowledged the influence of William Faulkner on his prose fiction, but since his poetry is grounded in the fundamental nondistinction of the two genres, a certain Faulknerian aspect of the poetry must be recognized as well. Two aspects of Faulkner's work are particularly important to Glissant: miscegenation and the consistent deconstruction of legitimacy and linear filiation (which in plantation cultures, as in Europe, was supposed to ground static systems of law and capital). Both are symptoms of the failure of Faulkner's characters to realize any real distinction between themselves and the prolixity of nature in the New World. Instead, despite nostalgic and ever (tragically) repeated efforts to define themselves in terms of European artifice, Faulkner's characters are always subsumed in a vegetal morass where impurity (miscegenation, *métissage, relation*) always prevails and no binarism (legitimate/illegitimate, artifice/nature) can survive.

DOMINANT THEMES AND IMAGES

The Sea

No image is more central in Glissant's poetic vision than that of the sea. It represents the bitter experience of expatriation, the long forced journey into exile of the slaves, as well as the enduring insight of accumulation and the nondistinction of humanity from nature *and* history. As he writes in *The Restless Earth:*

> The ancestor speaks, it is the ocean, it is a race that washed the continents with its veil of suffering; it says this race which is song, dew of song and the muffled perfume and the blue of the song, and its mouth is the song of all the mouths of foam; ocean! you permit, you are accomplice, maker of stars; how is it you do not open your wings into a voracious lung? And see! there remains only the sum of the song and the eternity of voice and childhood already of those who will inherit it. Because as far as suffering is concerned it belongs to all: everyone has its vigorous sand between their teeth. The ocean is patience, its wisdom is the tare of time.

The Land

There are three lands in Glissant's poetry: Europe, home of those who come to exploit the resources of the New World and subjugate its people, associated with linearity in thought and violence in action; Africa, the lost, longed-for origin of the slaves, the idealized object of negritude desire and absent motive of Cesairian fulguration; and the islands of the New World, the site of exile, loss, and rebirth, of knowledge bought by the painful "accumulation" of history. The unique geography of the islands has a special significance: defined on all sides by the sea with its shifting tides and borders of equally unsteady sand, rising out of the sea's fluidity and suspended in a state of never-quite-absolute distinction from it, the isles are characterized by a special intimacy with history and nature (whose difference the ocean suspends without ever quite dissolving) and by distance from both Africa and Europe. They are a place in which the difference between reality and imagination is never absolute.

Often the islands are characterized as a female figure, object of the conquistadors' desire, lover to the native people of the Caribbean who are killed by the Europeans "with only modicum of rage; with care." With "her" the displaced Africans ("I know a people down there in whom I shall trade . . . A people, O woman, who shall have you all night long for their pleasure and their pain") establish an intimacy of shared suffering at the hands of the Europeans, as in this passage from *The Indies,* spoken by the persona of a European explorer:

"Are you a fairy, whose gems I have known, and whose smile was the wind?
Are you this flame, outwardly peaceful, in which the wind held its wedding?
Are you this desire, more desirable than the woman of dawn, naked?
Are you, in this poem of myself who implore you, the poem of yourself,
   finally come?
O virgin! your lovers I shall kill with only modicum of rage; with care.
They adorn themselves with the gold of your breasts, and these jewels set fire
   to me!
I shall melt the gold, the part of you that I reserve for my kiss,
O virgin! here is the alchemist of your body, soldier of faith,
And he who loves you in a great wind of madness and blood, he is in you!
Come onto the bank of your soul! Hold out your treasures for your
   conquistadors!"

Conversely, Europe, in the person of the colonizer/conquistadors, is defined by its "phallic," totalizing desire to "possess" and "narrate" the "body" of the New World, not only by the figurative rape of the land but by literal rape/miscegenation with the enslaved Africans. The imagery used by Glissant to represent the "lust" of the Europeans is sometimes violent, as here, from *The Indies:*

"You deceived me, woman of this west! O inebriations! O torrents!
What may he drink now, the lover come from afar, what ardor, O moon?
I know the savage love that depopulates and uproots itself; it is mine!
So much sweat and ocean, to arrive at such desolation! Oh I shall stay!
And I shall rip to pieces your dung of jaguars and serpents! I, who entered
   through the Gate of the Sun!
I know a people down there in whom I shall trade; whom I shall hook up to
   your tit.
For your lovers whom I killed, stubborn love leads me to where are the heavy,
   crawling fish.
A people, O woman, who shall have you all night long for their pleasure and
   their pain.
At dawn, I shall scratch the black rind and make fall the secret dew.
So that my desire may assume durable form! So that the morning may belong
   to me, and the moon too!"
Now the earth wept, knowing what eternity is.

Errance

"Errance" ("wandering"), it will be remembered, is the movement of "accumulative" poetic consciousness, never static, always spatially and temporally displaced. It is evoked at times by the apparently effortless flight of birds in the island sky, but most often the topography of the shore is associated with Glissant's Persean poetic consciousness, while the hills and mountains (*mornes,* in the language of the islands) are linked to the explosive, phallic, and "fulgurative" poetics of Césaire and negritude. In between there lurks the lush, vegetal indirection of *errance,* blurring the boundaries between human and natural, felicitously contaminating every extreme with its opposite:

> [T]he savanna that spread farther and undulated between thin tufts of vetiver changed color with the wind; it seemed as virgin as the jungle born from the ebony trees, so that one was astonished to discover suddenly four or five houses lower down.[9]

The tree that grows on the island—"the tree of words feeding on a wounded shore"—in Glissant's poetry is a living embodiment of the poetic consciousness and its expression. "When I say: tree, and when I think of the tree, I never feel its singularity, the trunk, the mast of sap," he wrote in *Poétique de la relation;* "here the tree is the impulse, the Whole, a boiling density. When I try awkwardly to draw a tree: I end at a mass of vegetation, where only the sky of the page imposes limits on indeterminate growth. The singular is lost in this Entirety."[10] The poem-tree rises up out of the earth of language in *A Field of Islands:*

> Every word is an earth
> Whose subsoil must be searched
> Where a movable space is kept
> Burning, for what the tree says
>
> There sleep the tom-toms
> Sleeping, they dream of torches
> Their dream soughs in the tide
> Inside the subsoil of moderate words

This goes beyond using the tree as an organic metaphor of poetry. The poem literally unfurls from the poet like branches and leaves from roots and a trunk, and continues to grow and change; there is no concept of "completion" or closure, and we could scarcely be farther from the Parnassian ideal of the poem as perfect objet d'art:

> While you sleep in this plain, memory incurs the whirlings of the tree, and its higher blood. All prose becomes leaf and accumulates in the dark its bedazzledness. Make it leaf of your hands, make it prose of obscurity, and bedazzled by your breakings.

The tropical sun embodies the powerful force of subjective consciousness, which "doubles" the tree, casting its shadow onto the unpredictably shifting sand, in the specularity of self-awareness, the repetition of reading: "the light raises things up like the hand of an architect" *(A Field of Islands)*, as in this passage from *The Restless Earth:* "Delicious dangerous approach of noon. The tree's shadow is vertigo of naked soul which within itself consults and decides"; or, from the same poem:

> Country, when the rains take hold in the sun,
> Where the smithies of water braze a rainbow
> Man projects, after the storm, upon the Salt
> His taciturn shadow and his noiseless hope.

THE POEMS

Riveted Blood

Riveted Blood reflects Glissant's penchant for the fragmentary quite literally, according to Glissant: it is a collection of fragments, bits and pieces growing out of other works in which the pieces did not belong. Rather than a chronological sequence, it is a series of juxtaposed images. Its title anticipates that of his later work: blood is salty, and blackish when dried; the poem on the page is a fixed, or "riveted," residue of history, human suffering, and the poetic consciousness. Michael Dash observes astutely that these "poems are studded with words that refer to emanations from a natural order" (58). The images are also violent, and, as Dash says, often have to do with "altered states," expressing clear affinities with Rimbaud and Césaire.

Riveted Blood suggests immobility, and yet even dried blood remains mutable and organic. While the poem may appear to be fixed or "riveted" in place, it is a natural phenomenon, and its meanings and allusions, its very substance, are always shifting in motion—exactly, in Glissant's view, like History, which is always moving and changing even though it is in the past; *what is past is never finished,* what is done is never complete, what has been lost is always present, and the apparently fixed events of History are subsumed in a perpetual dance of changes. Time is just as illusory in fact as it is in literature. This is the phenomenon to which Glissant refers in the preface of *Riveted Blood* as "the effervescence of the earth." This destabilizing force defines our existence and makes us part of nature.

A Field of Islands

A Field of Islands observes the classical unity of time, describing the poet's imaginary vision from within a room through the course of one day. Throughout, the narrative voice of the poem represents a shifting locus of *errance* and *relation,* whose nonlinear progression is represented by the flight of a bird and the growth of a tree. Through the shifting perspectives of the poem, differences between the real (outside) islands and the poet's imagined vision of them, between the dilating movement of the poem and the growth of the vegetation outside, become blurred as the poet sees himself reflected in his own vision, which is not distinct from the real world outside:

> Here is the rebeginning of that clay in the heat of the heart, moving; a present time of islands harmonizing, O you! dreaming your face among them (beautiful, so beautiful). No one can say whether it is the surge of paths climbing up through pain, or if, from this night of solitudes and tides, it is pure asylum, starring into silex. No one may see or touch the half-day, touch the day with gentle hands. For itself, it establishes a wind of chestnut horses and of altitudes. Solidly, like someone thrusting his arm into earth, with the force of a sledgehammer. But also an elegance of molted bees, the wind clothing them with its tenderness. O this look [the poetic gaze] that from one to the next hesitates and accumulates!

Situating itself in an uncertain zone of dispersed, decentered subjectivity, the poetic voice avoids the first person, naming instead an absent "you" and a third person who often appears synonymous with the poet. The "clay that again moves, and climbs its own body" is both the poem itself and the real clay of the landscape, each a part of the other:

> You, escaped along the shores of day, easier bank than a pond's, whose round the tree [therefore the poem] tries in vain to compass. And he, fearless to enunciate his being in the embrasure, that he might be present, tousling expectation. O patience that flowers, undecided and yet firm and gentle, see if that is daybreak, gone astray in the bedroom? Or the harmony of disasters among the surge of paths? And this clay that again moves, and climbs its own body, did you light it, did you? Or maybe it's the sun, reentering the room, which all by itself placed this sad perfume of childhood in your eyes? O you, comprising memory and hope, opposite flowers, in this field of islands.

The poem contains frequent apostrophes to this "you," an absent woman, who in addition to being a real object of individual desire to the poet must embody the islands themselves, the poetic vision of them, as well as the lost land of origin, Africa, which is always like the woman here characterized by absence, and yet dispersed into every detail of the Caribbean topography and consciousness, present by its very absence. Yet often the "you" of the poem, the absent object of desire, seems to represent an aspect of the poet himself as he lives beyond the room in which he writes. Following this logic, the poet's desire would represent a nostalgia for totalization, the wish to realize a coherent totality out of all the poet's own disparate and decentered modes of experience ("memory" and "hope," nostalgia and expectation, the systole and diastole of desire):

> From this work, however, you are absent. Absent, who are there, like a bay! You get up, and it is as though one were seeing the sudden breath of air that takes shape and defies heavy flight of the gaze (beautiful, so beautiful). Absent who are every presence! . . . O you, absent from this work, but you alone are in it . . . O you, present in this work, yet is it not you who in the plain bewail the rootedness of your solitude, you know not, right down through there, in the leaves, this labor of mutations and legends, the tortured screech owl of language, the wave that unites its seaword with the earth, and the appetite of living in the midst of this fire! . . . Desire has gone away, where the fire goes to

suffer, and where, where, where? . . . Solemn, you smile at this desire, imbue it
with unchecked space. O absent one who are there. Thus he pushes his fields
toward the stranding sand, the heavy word.—And where now? he asks.

The impulsion toward possession and coherence is always gently deferred
by "stranding sand," the "heavy word," the natural unfurling movement
of the poem, in which even "absent" and "present" are not clearly distinct,
and there is no end to desire except more desire.

The Restless Earth

The Restless Earth is focused on the dialectic of sea and shore, from which
insight and knowledge arise. Here the poet is preoccupied by the suffer-
ing, which is the only route to truth:

> Immobile and immured earth
> In your silence, fragile
> There is but one place for truth
> Which takes pain, O doleful one

Sometimes gently, sometimes violently, but always leaving its mark of ero-
sion, the sea relentlessly by turns caresses and batters the sand of the shore,
shaping the traces, the topography of the poem/land that is never fixed. In
this poem, images blur the boundary between the sea and the land:

> All is naked, rich, save with enticements
> Toward the mass of lands I toil
> Oh I abandon the tides
> —Knowing you to be mystery

> And water's edge, when all is extinguished.

Here the edge, the shifting boundary of sea and sand, defines the real and
imaginary essence of the island, as well as the decentered poetic subject.
The same dispersal of subjectivity evident in *A Field of Islands* is reiterated,
the same use of second and third persons, the same image of the land as a
woman whose suffering seems to be the poet's own:

A cry of woman torn open
At the edge of the fallows
Her nubile breasts divided
Between misery and moss

Unique here is the section "Verses," which makes liberal use of the first person:

But I go back up into the fields and the storms which are roads of the country
    of knowledge,
Pure in the air of myself, and embolden myself with oblivion if the hail comes.

This section enacts the poetic subjectivity as a shifting locus, like the always moving line where the sea overlaps the sand, just beyond which rises the arboreal prolixity of the poem, neither mutable nor immutable but both at once and neither, like the tree and everything natural, existing without regard for such artificial binarisms: "A tree's faith neither lasts nor dies." The ephemeral point at which this dialectic of land and sea occurs defines the locus of poetic consciousness. The sea, with its indifference and perpetual depredations on the land ("The seafroth knows neither pain nor time"), is the agent of suffering, the road into exile, but this is what gives rise to understanding and the sense of nondifference from nature and what makes the joy of poetic insight possible:

I see this country as imaginary only because suffering,
And on the contrary, quite real, this is suffering before joy,
Seafroths!—barely there, they take fright and die. As we see:
"Upon the gravels, astonished with saltings,
A people walks within the tempest of its name!
And the fireflies accompany it."

The Indies

The long epic poem *The Indies* reinterprets the history of the New World and its discovery as poetical and imaginary phenomena. History for Glissant is always in flux, always shaping and being reshaped by the present, and the past can no more be thought of as "finished," representable in a format of precise chronologies and events, than can the future or the present.

The real meaning of the past lies in its shifting relation to the present. "The detailed reporting of dates and facts," Glissant wrote in *L'Intention poétique,* "masks from us the continuous movement of the past."[11] Here, the "Indies" are for the European explorers, as for the poet himself, an obscure object of desire whose reality cannot but clash with the idealized version of the Europeans: the "Indies" were so called because Columbus was seeking a westward passage to India and thought he had found it. Glissant's use of the word "Indies" and the consistent exclusion of "Caribbean" are not accidental; the poem's dramatic tension arises from the interval separating imagination and reality, desire and regret:

> *The imagination creates ever new Indies, for which men quarrel with the world. Those who left Spain and Portugal, lusting after gold and spices; but soldiers and mystics too. The Poem names Father Labat, Jacobin and corsair; then the Negro prophet whom he had whipped bloody, the one who had seen the boats burgeon on the sea, before they appeared; and names Toussaint-Louverture, slave and liberator of Haiti . . . but we must not get ahead of history: here, the port is on holiday, the adventure coalesces; the dream is exhausted by its own project. Man fears his desire at the moment of satisfying it.*

The Indies are a construction of European imagination before they are anything else, and the dream of them will never be separate from their reality, in Glissant's view. Confronted with the physical reality of the place they have traveled so far to find (or with what they think is the "Indies"), the Europeans' "language" of desire continues to pour out new metonymies:

> They have met the land, and step back into their history to consider it!
> They assemble on this beach, the virgin beach where is no mooring.
> They will start a market: of men and of gods—but the language ripens within them!—
> Of spices, gold, and yellow fever!

The poet's imagination of the land combines that of the slaves and their descendants, that of the land itself and its original, native inhabitants, and that of the Europeans.

The Indies comprises six parts: "The Call" (eighteen stanzas), "The Voyage" (fourteen stanzas), "The Conquest" (ten stanzas), "The Trade" (ten prose stanzas), "The Heroes" (twelve stanzas), and "Relation" (only one long stanza, the sixty-fifth). Each section is prefaced by a brief, unnumbered prose passage; all the rest of the poem is in verse, except for "The Trade," all of which is prose, serving to accentuate the unique horror of the Africans' experience during the slave trade. The poem contains all of the themes and personae of *A Field of Islands* and *The Restless Earth,* but these are developed in a less abstract format that combines lyric with narrative; it is probably the most accessible of all of Glissant's poetical works. As in the two earlier works, it recapitulates the image of the land as a woman who is raped by the Europeans, but without the poem ever turning into any sort of political manifesto. This is accomplished in part by the individual, human characterization of the land, the Europeans, the Africans, and all the other personae. These alternating and overlapping, often conflicting, visions of the islands all come together in the phenomenon of *relation,* which defines the place as well as the poet's vision of it:

> There is an Indies which finishes when reality brushes its arduous hair; a land of dream.
> It accepts what comes, suffering or joy, which is multiplicitous on the clay,
> (Halfway between each of the races, mixing them).
> From the dream described there, a high ground has come forth, which must be described,
> Its richness is to name every ferment and every ear of corn and wheat.
> Land born from itself, rain of the Indies they adopted.

Black Salt

Black Salt, published in 1960, is close to *The Indies* in some ways (its preoccupation with history and chronology, for instance, reflecting Glissant's predilection for narrative), but it also anticipates the denser, more opaquely lyrical poetry to come. History here extends beyond the European discovery of the Antilles to the ruins of Carthage, which the Romans buried in salt, through the commerce in salt that took Europeans to Africa, through to the Caribbean, where traces of this saline history wash up on the beach.

The title is densely allusive, referring both to the African diaspora and to the print on the page, which is the poem. The poem itself is as much an expression of nature as a tree, or as the sea's, dried residue on a shore-line: in the case of the poem, black deposits washed up on a white surface of paper from the depths of the poet's consciousness, which is a force of nature, like a volcano, a hurricane, or a vine—a force of nature that produces such residues just as plants grow and trees fruit. The title recalls that of René Depestre's *Mineral noir* (1956), but rejects the simply ideological and totalizing vision of Depestre in favor of something subtler and more self-consciously literary. In this respect the poem's title allies it to a later work of Saint-John Perse, *Amers* (Seamarks).

Yokes

Yokes originally contained an illustration by the Cuban artist Cárdenas that depicted a wooden yoke (a sort of collar placed around the neck of a mule or ox, to which a plow or cart would be attached) around an agglomeration of human bones. This may be Glissant's darkest poetical work. It was published during the period when he lived in Martinique and is a sequence of densely imagistic variations on the theme of limitation, ineluctable subjugation. It reflects Glissant's political concern for Martinique, whose unique cultural identity continued to erode under French rule, and the writer's own personal sense of frustrated containment. Stylistically, it is as dense and opaque as any of Glissant's writing before *The Great Chaoses*.

Dream Country, Real Country

Dream Country, Real Country is a meditation on the way in which what we call the real is shaped by human imagination, becoming finally indistinguishable from it—a distinctly Buddhist idea, though there are no allusions to Buddhist thought here. The poet sits in a quiet room, which is open to the island outside, and "constructs" the Antilles of his imagination and of the world beyond. Poetic consciousness is defined as the dialectical conversation or intermingling of these two things that are really only one, and the poem as the trace or residue of that conversation.

Fastes

In *Fastes* Glissant returns to his obsession with the fragmentary—and inscrutable—nature of experience. Each short poem is a riddle to which the answer is a place visited by Glissant. The sequence is thus a kind of geographical autobiography in the form of a series of riddles. It is most important to remember that "solving" the riddle—knowing the name of the place referred to—does not reveal or fix its meaning. That is always changing.

The Great Chaoses

The Great Chaoses is perhaps Glissant's most ambitious and most difficult work of poetry. In it, all of the themes and preoccupations that shape his previous work—poems, novels, and essays—find their densest and arguably their purest expression. It cannot be "read" in the conventional sense; rather, it must be allowed to pour over the reader like the waters of a great river, the Amazon or the Mississippi, both of which are explicitly evoked by the poem:

> *Off the Meschacebe, Father of Waters. The landscape, vertiginously horizontal, follows the course of the Atchafalaya River. It meets the one obstinate in heights and depths which in Martinique goes from Balata to Mount Pelée, by way of the Trace. Near to a primordial time, water and earth intermingled, in which the rhythm of voice is elemental: Here, measured in eight cadences. Everything melts into this sea and this earth: Mythology, the African night, the imaginary Vesuvius, the caribou of the North. The echo-world speaks indistinctly. The language of the island promises to harmonize with that of the continent, the archipelagic with dense spread-out prose. A disarticulated song in rigid stones, on the trace that leads from story to poem. Thus: "Boutou," baton of death, commander's instrument. "Grand-degorge," the native Caribbean who threw himself with all his own off a cliff, refusing Occupation . . . The lilies die, a fertile decomposition, by the grace of vanished deities. Commemoration of this water. Seizure of avenues.*

Such a poetry is inevitably difficult. Glissant has said:

> I even openly claim the right to obscurity, which is not enclosure, apartheid, or separation. The obscure is simply renouncing the false truths of transparencies. We have suffered greatly from the transparent models of high humanity, of degrees of civilization that must be ceaselessly worked through, of blinding Knowledge. This is the famous story of Voltaire who, while he was defending Calas, was buying stock in slave-trading enterprises. The transparency of the Enlightenment is finally misleading. We must reclaim the right to opacity. It is

not necessary to understand someone—in the [French] verb *to understand,*
there is the verb *to take*—in order to wish to live with them. When two people
stop loving, they usually say to each other, "I no longer understand you." As
though to love, it were necessary to understand, that is, to reduce the other to
transparency.[12]

But he is quick to distinguish between opacity and obscurantism: "Read a
poem. You don't need to understand it to like it. Worse, a poem under-
stood is a poem done with." So Glissant's poetry demands a different order
of readerly experience than mere comprehension, and to translate or to
read it calls for a different order of understanding, one that does not seek
transparency. Once the reader accepts that the poem is no more to be
made clear than the multicolored chaos of a Caribbean market street,
then the poem can begin to take on all the redolent, sweaty animation and
lively disorder of the real tropics, not the neat, static amusement park
reenactments of postcard and tourist brochure; the language of the poem
then begins to move around us like a hot night and resound in our ears
like the ocean at dawn. This is what Glissant's poetry does, if we let it.

In a recent interview published in *Le Nouvel Observateur,* Glissant said,
"I preach the return to poetry."[13] Indeed, arguably the most important,
at least the *purest* parts of his work are the volumes of poetry: *Riveted Blood*
(*Le Sang rivé,* 1947–50), *A Field of Islands* (*Un Champ d'îles,* 1952), *The Rest-
less Earth* (*La Terre inquiète,* 1954), *The Indies* (*Les Indes,* 1955), *Black Salt*
(*Le Sel noir,* 1960), *Yokes* (*Boises,* 1979), *Dream Country, Real Country* (*Pays
rêvé, pays réel,* 1985), *Fastes* (*Fastes,* 1991), *The Great Chaoses* (*Les Grands
Chaos,* 1993). (These dates do not agree with some published accounts but
have been provided by Glissant himself.) All of his poetry embraces the
aesthetic creed of the French symbolists Mallarmé and Rimbaud ("The
Poet must make himself into a seer"), and aims at nothing less than a
hallucinatory experience of imagination, in which the differences among
poem, reader, and referent dissolve into one immediate present experience.

I began this translation in 1993, thinking it would take me a couple of
years. It took ten, a large chunk of any writer's life. I am grateful to the
National Endowment for the Humanities, which awarded me a fellow-
ship to work on this project, and to Louisiana State University, which
supported my work in many ways. Several graduate students assisted
me during the time I worked on these translations, and I thank them

all: Rebecca Tebeau, Muriel Placet, Anne-Sophie Lamborelle, and Nabil Boudraa. The role of Melissa Manolas went far beyond assistance, all the way to a genuine and remarkable collaboration. It would be impossible to describe or express adequate appreciation for what she has contributed. My old friend and colleague Christopher L. Miller offered invaluable suggestions at a couple of points. The vision and judgment of Douglas Armato, director of the University of Minnesota Press, kept the project going through the long, lean years of hard work.

One final, essential caveat: in the process of translation, ambiguities that remain suspended in the original's solution must precipitate and, if the translation is to be any good at all, be resolved. Some violence is necessarily done to the original poem, no matter how subtly and carefully the re-solution occurs. The result is both a poem by the translator(s) and a reading of Glissant's poem at least as much as it is a poem by Glissant himself.

NOTES

1. Gilles Anquetil, "Éloge de la Peripherie," *Le Nouvel Observateur,* no. 1517 (February 1993).

2. Stéphane Mallarmé, *Crise de vers* (Crisis in poetry), in *Stéphane Mallarmé: Selected Poetry and Prose,* ed. Mary Ann Caws (New York: New Directions, 1982).

3. Édouard Glissant, *L'Intention poétique* (Paris: Seuil, 1969), 64.

4. Michael Dash, *Édouard Glissant* (Cambridge: Cambridge University Press, 1995), 30.

5. Glissant, *L'Intention poétique,* 49.

6. Ibid., 121.

7. Édouard Glissant, "Saint-John Perse et les Antilles," *La Nouvelle Revue Française,* no. 278 (February 1976): 68–74.

8. Dash, *Édouard Glissant,* 30.

9. Édouard Glissant, *Mahogany* (Paris: Gallimard, 1997), 252.

10. Édouard Glissant, *Poétique de la relation* (Paris: Gallimard, 1990), 80.

11. Glissant, *L'Intention poétique,* 187.

12. "Sur la trace d'Édouard Glissant," *Le Nouvel Observateur,* no. 1517 (February 1993).

13. Ibid.

THE COLLECTED POEMS
OF ÉDOUARD GLISSANT

RIVETED BLOOD

to every tortured geography

   Not work, taut, deaf, monotonous as a sea, endlessly sculpted—but eruptions yielding to earth's effervescence—that expose the heart, beyond worry and anguishes, to a stridency of beaches—always dislocated, always recovered, and beyond completion—not works but matter itself through which the work navigates—attached to and quickly discarded by some plan—first cries, innocent rumors, tired forms—untimely witnesses to this endeavor—perfectly fusing as their imperfections meet—persuading one to stop at the uncertain—that which trembles, wavers, and ceaselessly becomes—like a devastated land—scattered.

ONE SINGLE SEASON

Eyes Voice

    Torches confess to the black colored
pond of night
    Our liquid hands, our mood, earthy and depraved,
our eyes illuminated like burning straw!
    Seas, across you my silence patiently
awakens
    Beyond you are edges beyond you lie mud
    And the convergence of frost and defrost.

    The past the past
    Ah! stony memory rise up amid the stalks of cane.
    Each bush of memory conceals a sniper.

    Pounding a mill upon our heads
    Fires cough in our nights
    Whatever man does, the cry takes root.

November

And the oar is rooted in its waiting for a new land. Love for you, Oceania, is a rag tied to a mast, a coconut palm of fog at your side, Oceania in your shadow which is like a cathedral commemorating the uncivilized and I tame the waves of your robes Asia and Europe in our childhoods Asia a coral polyp living and feeding on itself, between sky and battle, while Europe is a field of nails. No longer hearing the rusted stream of wild butterflies on a thick day. Ever more fierce, the elections of assassins in the beautiful, cancerous rain. O the loveliest rain in which to pile up our skins, the loveliest O fingers of lianas in the brush of the ringing desert of Africa. The final mission was to mislead the word through the rich deafness of scorched Tropics. Like a summation of memory-intoxicated fruits in the mute desire of the banana trees.

Savage Reading

From a side of the mountain, the plain suddenly
thrusts the humble cart of its vastness into dazzlement
    In the mill of the factories my poverty smiles
at the powers of the earth
    In the scars of the sugarcane, in the still
black shinbones
    The water, so many times accosted, reddens at the touch
of my voice
    Emerging from the choleric depths of entanglement, here is
my leap into hesitation.

    Like hougans enfoliated with patience
    ah for proof I only seek the last
pilgrimage of my fatigue through the dry leaves of a
monsoon
    the flowering of islands, their frothy geography
in eviscerated seas
    our canticles, faces barred by springs,
our feet full of storms

    Cut, with your long stroke of dawn, cut where the
birds seek their nests in vain
    Through the rhythms of tom-toms the
earth reels despite me

    Like a gash, the winds bring forth from their flanks the weight of
shoulders into brilliance
    nights of recruitment for night.

NOTE

hougans: Priests of the voodoo cult.

Rock

Sea-foam, rain, head accosted by torrents of rainwater

O delivery of my faces luminous interlacing
knotted intersection of two rivers storm's auguries
I roll like a callus beneath the waves, the foam, I bathe
I a rock and the sea a rock, my bays are quiet, the
sea floods my presence
sea-foam, the landscape turns a convergence begins to germinate
the line of horizon goes back to the primordial place of my joy
trees dedicate the dry flight of their leaves to me
mud from ravines pours its
patient rumination toward my purity like a quay
quietly rots, silty tranquilities

And my senses joined my granular skin I exhale
my house my solitude Taoulo my thrashing voice
crushes Taoulo hisses

and the angry depth of the earth's womb raises up
its splendors around me
the rain-festooned air bears down upon me
its invisible restraints
Taoulo cries out, and next to me time lays down
its yellow scarves
and time steals invisible speed
the indolent putrescence of a wild mango on a rock.

Slow Train

The word I had nourished with fire kindled
from human flesh and lianas from the brush forest
   scrub brush that grows here in flesh exposed in
the sunlight of a clearing
   I have opened fiery pod of a louver, watching it with
my frozen orangutan eyes

   Land is when peacocks no longer dare to spread their tails
among boas and giant brambles
   Thinking of land I burst open the land as though
gathering splattered brains in the refuse of a new ocean
   rivers invent games in which my veins
are a hopscotch of fresh water for the fountains to drain
   I see myself as a child in the manger of an
earthly din of plunders and solitudes
   the sea carves out a friendship where I lay down my joy,
the word
   that swallows snow from streets like the armor
of a slave-ship
   They gave us amphorae in the iced
heart of this last day we slept in
torrents of moons we slept in the clouds
   They have carved us out driving tetanus
into the brush of our pores
   Of course the canals were dry and the astringent
bristle of rain melted into despair
   tremble house brine of rough diamond
   in the cage asleep
   fish

Tree Great Tree

    Your leaves are like the stale smell of desires
blind haymaking of the sea's arms
    Your foliage of medieval injury in the memory
of my splendors
    your branches are like the shoulders of a tilled woman on
the thirst of sharp grass
    your body is like a renewed tree from which I have loosened
the shell of my clarity
    your trunk of fresh leaves
    your trunk of light in the black field of
night-blooms
    your trunk of root that becomes trunk and
a marvel the bed of the creeping snail
    your sheaves your roots their frozen fire and
the masses of men gripping the teats of your
sorrows

    suffering like a winter in the wellspring of profundity.

Black Smoke

Mad madwoman breadless eyes, the blackbird's cry blooming
in its shadow of elderberry
  (it is the fourth star to the left following the
master's gaze)
  like a glazed street engraved upon the dizzying cataract
of totems.

LAVAS

Elements

Suns extinguished in the tresses of the true sun! I
shall take back the vitality of fruits aflame.

Here, on the trees, are knots of leaf-fed signs. The animals are my
friends in flesh. The rivers move through me toward the transparency of
lands I am there
In this infinite expanse of dew that young girls weave on their faces as
a declaration of love In
this murmuring that pirates braid into
clearings In this burgeoning of suns
dispersed by the trees' leafy wands It is I who am river,
opaque rock and within whose breast lies the fervor of
land
The thunderbolt the hand that caresses the lightning This willing
hand is us I have held in my fingers
night's shaggy hair I no longer sleep with spears pointed at my head
I no longer live on the cays near the caimans
bathing in cool water I study sand and the sky
opposes me with its glaucous gaze The shadows are
hostile to me Nothing less than splendor The melting
of waters and the dry neighing of seaweed

❧

You, who have struck up the sarabande and vertigo of the forests.
With candid gulps in your forest of stars you
erect the pyre of nights. In your forest resounds the
musical salvo of daybreak (my unknown life). In
full gulps, the land heaves us in imminence, beyond
the breathable waters of the poem you act out the sun,
and win. To sleep in the river to dig up the silence Leave
your hands in the shrubs of the Atlantic Between
mountains that July abruptly bursts O liberty

of tears in the land among the reconciled trees
And through the safety catch of suspended logic.

It is a country pounding its hips against the blindness Races races
arrows made of assegai canes Beneath the tambourine drum of baobabs
I snow and freeze
What others write
In capital stars
I feel it gently ruminate its own efflorescence and spread its many
compasses between my arms. Birds shoot like buds toward the crushed
thirst of volcanoes. Those who sew the white-threaded silence cannot
play the drunken game. I say that poetry is flesh.

And also, scraping with its only tooth (of storm blood tears), the great
ass-kisser acceptance. A jaw of sands, deserts, and brush, while the other
contains pollinated stars: may he expel the stars, broken-necked, the
whip the master who entombs and the canes that hiss with waiting, pain
and blood, his poetry and fury of poetry. Like the unfurling of unknown
tropic strata, dark fissure in the wind. Listen,
there are trumpetings,
leaning against the silence.
There is an infernal dew among the clearings of sea-salt
In the sap and brilliance I have slowly poured both green and red water,
harvested murderers canes and gourds Drink up The sun is a lantern,
targeted and vanquished Splendors, pilgrims of the sea-foam!
My home braided in defiance toward the lightning, reeds that elude
October's hougans, my home my sea-prism home America's long barrier.
The rebel blacklisted for teaching children that a hand has but one
finger. I brew the thicket of waves. My waking is the dog dragging its
shelter beneath the bridges.
Errancy ensnared, made obsolete
when when and when the emaciated
bells of the inaudible?

Yet I am present in history down to the marrow. Embedded secularly:
in this afternoon which I have uttered as vigorously as ignorance: it
moves its gravel within me. I wait, eating poetry, roses Yes
    I am measured piece by piece
    in nocturnal
    music.
Man coolie-sailor sea-foam Ah the dew of my hair that you mistook for a
surge of coralline mucus Not a voice but a murmur Drilled-built Negroes
    not killed incinerated decapitated but lynched I move about in the
embers
Other forces are coated with my strength! Clowns, who only now rise.
A beautiful disgrace. Here to testify to virtuous splendor in the name of
poetic plagiarism. I must salute: man, this luminous desire of song.
Vocative, exceedingly so.

The forest suddenly howls at life. Stars and vagrants raid the sluices.
Vibrant oh vibrant, queen. Your feet follow the path of abandoned
mango trees. Your skin turned inside out is a plowed field of red.
Vibrant,
    O my vibrant prairie morning you my prairie-night raped by the
bullfight. You slipped in the water the sighs of your silhouette cut from
glass. The ford at the black beach black sand of touches. In the star
beautiful star of your hands. Tranquil pounding of dawns in the
scorched nave of your dreams, your voice of accosted brilliance, of husk
mixed with husk: I suspend the storm upon the recess of your lips.
    Ah sudden is
    the fear of being two
    in beauty

Your lightning a mane of snows your lightning both air and love
interlaced. You, serpent and furrowed. I, sea-foam of your footsteps.

And so I was, colony of children martyrs of lost dogs of unconverted
dogfish. O suffering, this beating of wind in the streets. Poverty is
ignorance of the land, passion is that which is imagined.

But there has been no rustling, nor sun, as long as man's singular opened mouth has waited. Let us proceed to other continents.
    Stirring rock
    Man ravaged alive, tillage
    Tainted storm, O
    wondrous chalice, for you I am blood. Roots, roots, I will never stop tugging at your fertile teats.

Fire has chosen to envelop me with what I thought was the last wave.

Nourishing Air

Within the snare of the horizon lies a grip that unravels childhood the mysterious
    man intoxicates himself with my white cruelty the one I inhabit the one offering me his visage of gradual inundation the one who grants me his cities or simply his agony making me more beautiful than an apparition of tears in a valley more beautiful than a weeping valley between three blasts of death's trumpet I am in the tower of silence like a white bird

From seas within seas through the sweetness of nitrogen retracing its way back to the water's threshold beautiful visitor
    Delicate lather of rains the accumulation of dews
    Nothing but me volcanoes drain their exposed bloody teats before me why
    except that I arrive within me there is air impregnated with the atmosphere of torture of oblique persistence

and I crawl through a recurrence of dawns of afternoons farther away my dead brothers exchanged for dead stars (in the space lie the shreds of your flesh) you males females and permeable and equal and unequal

You seas in your hands are so many failed shipwrecks you men you serpents you cities gauging depths in the entrails of the land do not harrow me with your beacons
    I erupt worlds worlds into space

Emptiness is a steaming bowl a morning of plunder
Oh to live at the throat of thieving emptiness
In the derisive river a flight of sparrows
At my shoulders by my sides one day
The earth will cease to turn within the prison of which it speaks

And though you may try, captain, the gymnastics of red irons upon my lips will never drive me toward this bread stamped by the discounting of my flesh,

Rain holds you among the islands, slaveship-surveyors of the Atlantic,
so many storms have dared to record for us the putrid air of your passing
   rain, keeper of secrets, imbues me with the smell of a numbing song
fern of rains upon my back mangled sheets of rains upon my hands
against the pied scars burning feet the too complicit sea

   Through tunnels which illumine saps and the eye continues to
rummage through the starry streets of sap-burned roots
   I wait for the pooled waters' drill softened by water and shining its
light against the nostrils of mules, their ears pricked to the sound of its
grinding rain and sun fused

   The only body I have is the one released for the raining of
underground trysts O shower of craters engraved with green prolixity
   Plowing its worlds among me.

   Mimosas have closed the rivers' pulp beneath the wing of sparrows
   A magister for once, I reconcile unrelenting suns the whiteness of
streets
   O singers blocked in assaults from the sky, you, stars hurled toward
them

   Through the mountain I hear sentient caverns (nostrils and acoustics)
I hear metallic fragrances solemn mendicancies
   The blind man eats his bread, the tree leans against its double

   Because beautiful the poem imposed upon the late hour the
plowshare of heat-strokes within the fallowness of napes.
   Billions of stars from the manchineel tree milk boiling in the cool
of eyes.

MIRRORS

Cities

Some object of silence upon the wool of noise, but one so vast.

It consists of love, of its movement towards meticulous shop windows.

Who stops and contemplates? Here thought organizes the display of rags and charm lingers indefinitely.

There, enormous cats scratch the earth, steel of silence and belief without purpose.

Confession

Every face is a cry a shattered mirror
Weighing in its hands the despair
Before it, trembling as silence encroaches

This is how the confession blooms.

There is not space enough for these hands
Nor a trace of friendship,
Secret, so secret.
Who dares say if his face
Clings to his body or if the mask of it
Is transparent?

Mirror, through which nothing passes O cliff.

She is a bird, pure movement
Consumed by wind.

Have they piled up their loves
Soul upon soul like
Marl or peat or chalk deposits
Cheap laborers stalked by the wind

Out of terror the apothecary
In his minefield lit sparks,
Rings worn by dead women
For a forgotten dead man

See, the poor winnower
He wove the wicker of caresses
The reposed will have no rest
Without the mirror being tarnished by it.

The one who tortures is hidden in many places by the road
He instills, contaminates
Offends and rises through himself
So he may attack in absolute silence.

The solitude that moves him dies away
He brings the sea near, he scolds
The vanquished remain, a dispersed and occulted confession.

Vertigo in Cold Weather

Ashes cane stalks O your days
Are abandoned by the infinite
Like fine clothes your lies
are lamentations, animated by a mirror

Frail mirror and lofty tower
Water of death, which is confined
to no ocean beyond tilling
Furrowed fever and clay

Weep so that my space may bind
Upon you a space more absolute
Than an ocean upon an exile

My fevers cultivate the dead cane stalks
For such lies become ash once more
And clay beyond infinity.

SEASONS

Glory

for Jacques Charpier

Queens of the new azure rise from their countries, unbridled.
River of flora, and morning's path,
From the dawn itself, from the blue, and horses neighing,
I saw you made glorious and sad by antiquated words,
And this mirage this embrace,
Mares now familiar, and tamed.

And, like a druid in a ghostly forest of the past, you welcomed
An afternoon. There, time and future were wed, their nuptial warmed
you.

Flames. Charges at the gates of noon. May this entire
song
Of soils and rivers descending the plumb of day
May you become a place of order, of thirst, not of feasting or abrupt
blindness
And may this lure not lead you to cling to the desperate evergreen of
olden times.

To Die, Not to Die

for Jean Laude

Fragrances have withered on the beaches of my stars. The foams from above no longer dazzle, the book remains there, along with its harvest.

A book of walks where water is scarce, a book of the Dead and Lethes, in this northern land occupied by vineyards, underground oh under the ground.

Open, for the nights are splendid in this Book. (The sea measured its fruits and salt. Summer was illumined by the summer of night.)

I learn I learn that there is a battle, after which love never returns, for it is dead; and the field is deserted, there was no combatant there, but only a solitary and eternal defeat.

And see the water used to cleanse the dead; the wife smeared it beneath footsteps of the clergy.
Death and its ferrymen are renounced
For leaving at core this immense sea that is always starting over.

Temptations

for Paul Mayer

Lassos you leave us in the white day whiter than the summer's snow
  Blind ones, upon your bodies move dreams of the past, there you
bind salt with so many unbound storms

  In love words burst into flames and tear apart
you wander
  For you love infringes upon the sky and you have only depths
  And only caves and cliffs for your desperate bodies

  In plowing you linger and are snow beneath the icy rind
  What do you say as you sleep beneath the thickness and within the
fiber
  You who so disturb and delight us?
  Or are you merely ghosts inhabited by ripples of impurity
  Or are you only lassos to entangle yourselves, in order to bruise and
tempt us?

Solitude

for Roger Giroux

Mast that the snow has bound with silence
At the beach where suddenly there is no longer salt
He recognizes the sea ruptures the shore's face
And escapes the wind where moons fall in love.

Night comes it comes and rises up like a white coral
On the breast aroused by a wind of prophecies
She unearths not a vessel of furies nor of blue love
But an absence of light.

O perfection of defeat O law of morning
The solitary wind has entwined the wave and given it back
A sweetness in the chalice of its body
And like a son to caress.

Daughters of the sea! Men of salt! Gods auspicious to feasts!
O nuptials that never cease.

Beauty

for Max Clarac-Sérou

Here is a wind of solemn roses it is azure
Weaving into a flowering of irrealities, such beautiful hands
This is summer stripped of its dream by the wind, the naked child
Weeping before the daylight, awaiting noon.

Your city understands you. Hardly a word beseeches this
Invisible breeze more secret in its sap and unspeakable
Compelling us to boast of transparencies. See,
   Salt mends the season, the auburn trees, the child.

Roses of irreality, we shall name the impure incense.

FROSTS

Abrupt

No song or spectacle on your deserted plain
But innocence fallen crimson
Obituary sediment layered within your death
A laugh so let a dead man bury his wound in the sand
A cry a knot a weighty plumb of fallen heads
No song
But this stone in your hand where the wind cries
And wounded birds fruits and words dream
While you abruptly ambush
Blood riveted and vigorous in a windless night

Mainstay

Sampan there were too many paths and a jungle in the horizon there were a thousand black chalks beneath the mirror a wound there were how many tears a bay

Sampan in the evening the tears and chalks came back to us in the horizon through your passages there was a single mirror for this wound and our bay beneath the jungle

Sampan dreaming (born dying) we hailed you as our forest there was the osprey's cross and your vastness for our dreams and your oath upon our lips

Here is the mainstay who now approaching and evading gives us the year wherein everything appears (like a smile that stalks and seizes us even as we are born).

The Dead and Living Tree

All night at the edge of the horizon
He sought you, not daring to shout above the gold
Whether you cried out among dead birds
Or gave voice to the people
Or arrived speechless in the windows' thickness.

He clung to night among the trees
He rose in its dawn and death
He dearly loved so much shadow he banished the noise
And righted you, pure you in whose hands flowed
the midnight lavas that we contemplate within a tree.

He held himself before the night
Supported by a glacial wind
While city-less eagles rose

Fallen beggars bathing the horizon.

A FIELD OF ISLANDS

I

Torments, sea fire, pitiless expanses: these are the high margins of coal
mines, sometimes the wind that gently stirs, gently surprises the heart
and adorns it; these are packs of wolfwinds that fly out of hands, toward
sin and the accomplishment of gravel. These cavaliers fall in love with a
liana, hearing that it sprouts through the sky unto the utmost stars! Oh
out of this language that is every stone, enfleshed and raising flesh up
over itself, out of this violent and gently obscure language that is the
root, endowed with flesh and pushing flesh underneath itself, here is the
rough draft. It is not at all the heat of the word giving off sparks, but
peoplings of hands beneath the skin: the massive crime of the corolla
at its edges of pink pond, and the rising of folluaries, and falling
feathertrain of birds of paradise. What can be this cry, this shatter of
panes in the voice!—may the day abruptly depart, deflowering, from this
room where you are coiled around the sails of life, toward this language
that loses itself, and then takes itself back again? It situates your
night-afflicted hands in the island. Under the somber foliations of frail
skin you send forth your smile like a bird of the seashore; this is the
thunderclap of your silence, the tranquil prose of your hands that make
light out of the world, and conquered it between its hedgerows.

Here is the rebeginning of that clay in the heat of the heart, moving; a
present time of islands harmonizing, O you! dreaming your face among
them (beautiful, so beautiful). No one can say whether it is the surge of
paths climbing up through pain, or if, from this night of solitudes and
tides, it is pure asylum, starring into silex. No one may see or touch the
half-day, touch the day with gentle hands. For itself, it establishes a wind
of chestnut horses and of altitudes. Solidly, like someone thrusting his
arm into earth, with the force of a sledgehammer. But also an elegance
of molted bees, the wind clothing them with its tenderness. O this look
that from one to the next hesitates and accumulates! You, escaped along
the shores of day, easier bank than a pond's, whose round the tree tries
in vain to compass. And he, fearless to enunciate his being in the
embrasure, that he might be present, tousling expectation. O patience
that flowers, undecided and yet firm and gentle, see if that is daybreak,

gone astray in the bedroom? Or the harmony of disasters among the surge of paths? And this clay that again moves, and climbs its own body, did you light it, did you? Or maybe it's the sun, reentering the room, which all by itself placed this sad perfume of childhood in your eyes? O you, comprising memory and hope, opposite flowers, in this field of islands.

This day!—in which, equaling the Mountain nearer than a knot of lamps on your forehead, he raised you up in him through the snows, aerating you with a large discourse of opals, of sensitive plants. Patience has grown large in absence, wounded by his absence and the presence of another voice, not yours, and of you, upsetting your towers of despair, purifying the other (and not him) with your sweetnesses. Since that day, the light has advanced with a terrible stride, the earth is a past of nevadas, a High Plain of wanderings on their ninepins. This clay moves again! Could it be that the bird guides the sky toward a spring? Could it be, very far off, the embarking of banks of snow toward a burned-out crowd? Or the heart, is it the heart, agitated like a train-station of vegetal populations, which smokes upon the city its sweat of earths, its tumultuous surf? No one confesses, no one can, that this childhood is the hurdy-gurdy of a bivouac. And he, he no longer fears the affection (of naming himself "I" in this earth), but rather sows it with wheat and plants it. And you, hardly guessing all this stir of stars and ivy, profuse in this language, indifferent and sudden calm in the fruit, you make mystery just as he does, from the silence where the city rustles. To reach your daylight (as one might attack pain, burning it all the way to its stars), here is the clay commuted, this fruit bestirred, the sweet screech owl of language. Naked furors, lances of air, forests O multitude! which your faith comes to ravish, in this field of uninvented islands.

From this work, however, you are absent. Absent, who are there, like a bay! You get up, and it is as though one were seeing the sudden breath of air that takes shape and defies heavy flight of the gaze (beautiful, so beautiful). Absent who are every presence! When you walk upon the horizon, the blood that walks in the earth finally rests and becomes a spring at the extremity of thickets. You smile so gravely that water comes back to you; and that spring has unbridled the eternity of light. O you, absent from this work, but you alone are in it. While you sleep in this plain, memory incurs the whirlings of the tree, and its higher blood. All prose becomes leaf and accumulates in the dark its bedazzledness. Make it leaf of your hands, make it prose of obscurity, and bedazzled by your breakings. O you, present in this work, yet is it not you who in the plain bewail the rootedness of your solitude, you know not, right down through there, in the leaves, this labor of mutations and legends, the tortured screech owl of language, the wave that unites its seaword with the earth, and the appetite of living in the midst of this fire!—make it flamboyance of indecision, may the heart be a presence of clarities (no one admits it). See excess and moderation, hearths without end, in this assent of horizon. When you walk on the horizon, the chamber disassembled here lets out its water, your conviction. Desire has gone away, where the fire goes to suffer, and where, where, where? . . . Solemn, you smile at this desire, imbue it with unchecked space. O absent one who are there. Thus he pushes his fields toward the stranding sand, the heavy word.—And where now? he asks.

Let all this place be mute like an orchardless poem, or let this tree hesitate at the edge of you, looking for the bird with its gaze embroidered upon you, the nave of high trees upon the height, and the pointed arch braided out of shadow for your bending—is not all splendor mute? As a poem hesitates at the water's edge, gropes with the foot watches for the ford reflects the sky in its fordless hazes, fordless! as a poem of masts and spars cries out its sail and its topsails,—thus does he remain at the frontier of you, marauder from another country, a rock on his forehead as a sign of ancientness. Who is late in saying what cannot be said, he establishes himself in the dawn. He whom opacity troubles, who divines childhood, he grows in the assurance of his voice, the clumsiness of his feet,—the slightest wind makes him yield. What would he say, if you know, or even if you don't know, O immensity upon toil? Forever the fiber of your gaze, foreign to the fiber of his, forever. The grass where you bathe, girlchild promised to the plenitudes of earth, in vain upon his roots would he try to raise it. (Or shall you

remain disconsolate upon your sand, purifying thirst and hunger?) Here
for a long time another sky, another bay, may he endure there forever.
Another harvest, may he raise from it his leavening. And, upon the
landings of your body, may he enfeeble his waiting (another patience,
another shower of rain), it matters not. His silence is to call you to the
foliage of grandeur where the sea is born, and after it the continents, and
all flavors divvied up beneath the blade of light, spectral layers of silence,
vultures and whitenesses of cry, and every thing in bloom toward its
daily island, open, calling, and secretly closed, and mute as any splendor.

You, presence, anxiety of stone, work of sun when it is lizard on rock.
Oh your presence is of day, its miraculous wrong side, clumsy. And if
the breath hesitates, it is a good sign. Moors, leavenings of morning.
Roadways satiated, once the gully of language is crossed. Your absence,
like rain, opens the light; infinite, after the circumscribed intimacy of
each form; guardian of word in the secret alleyway. Oh here again is the
field of day and night, assumptions, one of flesh and then the other of
singularity. It is not absence of any season that is effaced by the return
and the unmindful reunion. It is not the presence of reason, the pathway
of dialogues, the hand in the heart like a splice of glory. Red acacias
upon dream. Voluble blood along the way! Absent, she who is presence!
That the word yet hesitates at the poem's threshold, ripens in the deepest
depths display of their approaching nuptials, this is testimonial for the
bridegroom. Oh it is not at all absence, nor half-presence, but so full
that being is to them as a furrow of earth. All flesh divides, at dawn and
at evening, from presence and from absence, for fire and for weaning.
O mango tree, image of its succulences! Bedroom of evening, lullaby of
nightjar, and your white statue's head, so very white! All day long this
image has pushed its tidy lips like a shore. Now that evening is here,
bedroom of evening, lullaby of nightjar, place yourself upon the crest
and expand your dream. But expanding it up to the heights of this
absence, under the ribbed vault of filaos, bring it back yet again to the
stubborn faith of this presence, amid the crowd!—O poem born of you,
who are born to the whole world's toil.

2

To know what within your eyes cradles
A bay of sky a bird
The sea, a devolved caress
The sun returned here

Beauty of space or hostage
Of tentacular future
Every word is lost there
In the silence of Waters

Beauty of ages for a mirage
The time that remains is for waiting
The time that soars is a cyclone
Where it is the road, scattered

The afternoon has veiled itself
With lianas of emphasis and frozen
Fury, with volcanoes brought
Hand in hand beside the sands

The evening germinates in turn
Within the country of pain
A hand that dissolves Evening
In turn shall gently fall

Beauty of waiting Beauty of waves
The waiting is almost a bowsprit
Interwoven with wings and winds
Like a confused jumble on the bank

Every word comes without one having even
Scarcely to budge the horizon
The landscape is an abrupt sieve
Of words pushed under the moon

To know what upon your haggard hair
Tries on its harness for the first time
And the salt, does it come from the sea
Or from that voice that circulates

Abandoned are the whirlings
Of adventure on the drums
The assault of blood in the plains
Its foam on the Heights

Abandoned, the well of suffering
The suffering just off the sky bears away
Into the crowd of kapok-trees
Its wolfpack of words and its prey

Abandoned dried up the moderation
Immoderation of cutlasses
This music is to the heart
Like a hamlet of lassitude

Beauty rarer than in the island
Your great pathway of stupefaction
Is it going to bury your gaze
In the sweet humid earth

Men come out of the earth
With their too strong faces
And the appetite of their gazes
Upon the sails of clearings

The women walk before them
The whole island is soon woman
Full of pity for herself but clenching
Her despair in her naked heart

And among the cries of noon
Ravined with triumphal sweats
Upon a horse there comes to pass
The deceased woman, tomorrow Pity

The entire island is a pity
Which upon oneself commits suicide
In this accumulation of assaulted clay
Oh the earth advances its virgins

Filled with pity, this island, and pitiable
It lives on words derived
Like a halo of shipwrecked people
Searching for rocks

She needs words that last
And make the sky and the horizon
More indistinct than the eyes of women
More clear than the gazes of a solitary man

These are the words of Moderation
And the hardly silenced drum
In the innermost depths henceforth stirs
Its waiting for other shores

The afternoon the Evening the hovels
The fist stuck in the hard wood
That hand that decorated pain with flowers
And the hand that raised the horizon

Upon your paths what song
Was able to defend the clarity
Upon your eyes that love burned
What earth has deposited itself

Overseas is the chastity
Of incendiaries in books
But the fire in the real and the day
Is the courage of the living

They make the bird they make the foam
And the house of lava sometimes
They make the opulence of ditches
And the harvest of the past

They obey their hands
Manufacturing echoes without number
And the sky and its purity flee
This purity of rockwork

They make the earths that make them
The futures that spare them
Oh the filaos exalt them
Upon the crests of memory

Mules snakes and mongooses
Make these men violent and gentle
And the light blinds them
The night at the edge of the colonial highways

Every word is an earth
Whose subsoil must be searched
Where a movable space is kept
Burning, for what the tree says

There sleep the tom-toms
Sleeping, they dream of torches
Their dream soughs in the tide
Inside the subsoil of moderate words

Their dream cradles your eyes
Panics and maelstroms
More agitated than the deep outback
When the light passes saying

Sanguine beauty of gulfs
Oh it is a wound, a wound
In which dances the sky, solemn and slow
To see men naked and such

And the whole island finally reposes
In the heat of ripeness
Ripe is the silence upon the city
Ripe the star in hunger

That which rocks in your eyes its song
Is the adornment of herds
The bullgrass for foremasts
The hard reflection of salts in the south

Nothing distracts lives from order
Men walk children laugh
Here the earth is loaded with supplies, consenting
With currents of water, with sails

What stiff thought traverses
The fibers the saps the muscles
Of pain have we made a word
A new word which multiplies

He who engenders among the snows
A landscape a city thirsts
He who arranges his drums and cloths
In the sandness of words

Awaiting the opening of Boundless Waters
The great glitter of Meridional waves
More burning than the bite of frosts
More restrained than your thorny impatience

Who is prolonged by waiting
And all the hands in his head
And all splendors in his night
That the earth might be astonished

He accepts the noise of words
More identical than the dread of springs
More uniform than the flesh of plains
Torn into pieces filled with seed

Its clarity is in the ocean
In the patience that is dragged
Toward where no eye may strain
By the flora of oriental islands

That which cradles its song in your eyes
To reach the morning O intimate
Yet unknown one, this is the wild heat
Of Chaos where the eye at last touches

Island these sharks your manuring
The cartage of your blood the man
And his hillock the woman and the huts
The avenue in these mirrors the Hands

Is it bird, a root that spurts
Is it harvest, friendship grown out of the earth
The same color splashes, caresses
The suffering is not to see

Beauty of this people of magnets
Among the vegetal filings and you
I circle you like the ocean
With its manure of wrecks

Beauty of multicolored highways
In the savanna that ruminates
The storm full of words that will hatch
I lead you to your threshold

Listening to my drums streaming
Awaiting the sudden crash of billowblades
The awakening of dancers on the water
And of dogs who look from between legs

In this noise of fraternity
The stone and its lichen my word
Just but keen for you tomorrow
Such fury in the sea's mildness,

I make myself into ocean where the child shall dream.

3

Oh all this place is dead, more so than dawn within bedrooms, far from wind. Nevermore shall the wind go by the word, sending dreams on their way. The evening is a basin of brush, of dirty roses. This wind is no longer the arena where plovers gambol! Nevermore, oh never shall dawn go forth saying dawn, "I am the awakening of eyes and the light of depths." And he in his deepest depths no longer stirs clays, or reveling populations. Did he used to say only, like the dawn, "I," in this dread of promenades?—no one knows. Oh the prow of middays drummed on his heart. Perhaps you have felt the pathos of seashores at midday? Perhaps you are there, in the fissured voice, that wintry birth? But he no longer touches anything except the ramshackle houses of this noise around the streets where the grass grows. It grows! straight and bloody in his heart (is it in the street, or in his heart?); straight and high and wounded, the grass has climbed up onto night! Now upon the prairie the handsome plovers have returned and make streetlamps, no, stars. What is a star but that very obscure, humble thing, that he sets afire and throws through his strength and his despair, forever fixed? What is power, tell me, if not despair when he takes hold of his body and flings himself in the grass, so the grass grows? No one admits it, but he knows what is the sap in the stem. And you, do you know it, this wound whereby the word oozes from the trunk, splitting the bark? Word of whiteness, no landscape, no branch.

Extinguished gazes, beneath the appearance of blue water . . . Live, seabirds, within the smile, and describe the orbits for his laughter. Oh the sadness, leaving its own banks to establish other countries! So the blood circulates into the untuned galleries, a hand fails to resume the heat of stars for its pleasure, the word comes undone, it is a blast of cold lavas. Undone, abandoned, drifting upon hope, flower, flower and patience, it goes down the banks. On the banks: scuffles, cities, upright girls cry out to the passing day. All that was pure becomes confused and choked with brush. Here it is that he goes back up the soul of the river, toiling toward earthquakes. Toward that chaos to carry thunderous words. And where the words are to be reborn in surges, such heavy

fields! All that was keen, becomes torrid; all,—of bad brick, is
intertwined. In vain would he keep the rhythm of paddles in the
current. His word is awkward, its colors exhausted. His word is sealed
with thorns, the wind is no longer from favorable araucaria tree, which
moves. Remember, there were immense celebrations on the banks!
And the filthy day had brushed against the water of you both, without
blemishing the living water.

Shall he take root in the unknown, shall he erase himself in pain like
one who sings? Fervors were next to lakes in your face—the sky worried
for stars it already missed. So he conducted wedding parties to their
harbor. This bird flew away from him, as though from a fruit. What cry
is this, oh which, if not that of the only disentwined country? He carried
upon hope these names of the seas: islands distinctly pronounced,
muttered archipelagoes, continents (a deaf sound), saying, "For you I
open up these shores . . ." And wishing, "This clay take me," he rose up
from the Conflagration, April with his words. See him, see him drifting
in such riverine splendors. His words, his thorns, or maybe rocks, so
awkward, badly cut. O Whitenesses, in which the sky is without islands!
See him land on that brazier as the pink flamingo (lost on the seas)
might rest without resting, upon typhoons and tumults. From whence
does she come, suscitated, but so alien? Like an illicit horizon? And did
he not used to say, so long ago, "I do not love this woman," without
truly realizing whether he was still speaking of a woman, or (so empty
and sly was the waiting) rather of this abused and deluded earth, there,
where blood grows like a cry? . . . Now the sands are of another light.
One must choose, one must come! either by the sea, known to the
kingfishers, with their funereal dreams, or in the earth, black and
naked trunk . . . And then, did you know it, this project of building
the landscape?—sometimes the heart is crushed, the air is hostile;
sometimes the hand is assuaged—and the light raises things up like the
hand of an architect.

Whitenesses! moistnesses of the word that does not question! Snowy
fever, ornaments! Whiteness that passes by and that erects. It reappears

in his life, when this voice assails him. He capitulates in his life which is again upright within him, but his word is on guard like a holiday rosebush. Ah! Will I finally have to come back and name, knowing that the same is true of me as of the tree after the wind? And you, scarcely guessing this cry of bloods that have been stirred, this river flowing along you, life hailed by quakings—shall I have to name you in order that the island may live (in you)? Is it lava, blood, uproar, sap of noise, or the wind, these processions? Is it the wind, the immobile horror of things (but see how the word has already come back white), furors beneath the skin and crowds? The time shall come of capitals—where is the crowd set afire,—or else the sun is made of snow! Thus, forcing the wavefoam, I shall go along the beaches where the word dies, suddenly just. See how the word has lost some of its whips, some of its blacknesses. Where are the islands? Who is piling up the cuttings? . . . There will be crispations, and the drunken songs of hedgerows. Smiles, the hand that offers, bright time. And what presence now, I ask? Nonetheless I search, heavy and burning.

THE RESTLESS EARTH

MOVEMENT, FAR FROM SHORES

Theater

Who is exhausting this instant?
Already the sky is heavier than the bifid water in the dawn,
The rain, the rain staggers
I know you you are bank and beyond it mystery.

Oh the beacons of the forest, oh the organs of the immured water, You,
Calyx of my knowledge, stamen on the plain, storm almost, in the evening
O riverine clan!

As a flower keeps itself impure
As a city laments
Nature Nature
Who can cure it of its torments?

The rain has closed its curtains against the cheek of the fields
I do not know if it is the city or the nice weather,
But all things come together and congratulate,
Exchange vows of beautiful love.
I know you who are bank and beyond it mystery.
The rain,
Having scolded just as at the moment of the curtain,
Begins its dialogue with earth, of water.

Ocean

The ancestor speaks, it is the ocean, it is a race that washed the continents with its veil of suffering; it says this race which is song, dew of song and the muffled perfume and the blue of the song, and its mouth is the song of all the mouths of foam; ocean! you permit, you are accomplice, maker of stars; how is it you do not open your wings into a voracious lung? And see! there remains only the sum of the song and the eternity of voice and childhood already of those who will inherit it. Because as far as suffering is concerned it belongs to all: everyone has its vigorous sand between their teeth. The ocean is patience, its wisdom is the tare of time.

Incantation

"Listen, I discover you and consider, I am just. So much snow. However I was from another lava, O tranquil ones."

—In the mid-morning, scarcely even a lighthouse made from shade the cathedral of its flight.

"See my wounds and the scars of my wounds. See my storms, my flux. I am still dying, you passersby."

—O brush O ravines O crowds O bruised ones.

Oh the countries without substance and the pale nights!

THE RESTLESS EARTH

for Jacqueline Baldi

Morning

Your fields die, your endless fields:
From branch to branch toward the echo
The dream is hardly in the flower
Already the wind runs to morning.

A man weeps with beautiful teeth
Humble, loitering dogs sniff him
He mediates body adrift
In the clearing of the crowd.

Is he, at the edge of the wreck
A place of lavas where the dawn snows
Through its inordinate birds,

As one sees brightnesses in May
As a calming of tides
Or as flowers here are shallow waves.

The Bay of the Sky

She, mirror, and so guarded
That the atrocious grasses flee
Where go the waiting and the torture.
Tree clings not in the hollow hand of path
That in old age becomes road.

She has budded, woman on the water
Immobile on the surface, seaweed
Naked, avowal of air which for pleasure turns itself to storm.

Secret Cliff

I

Did he think of the books buried
In these countries without spectacles
Where women no longer have hands?
These fulgurations of rocks
That we see along the naked shores
Over waves yet keep watch?

The sea had engulfed him
From edge to edge in its love.

II

The ill wreaked by the wounded bird
On the cloud that finishes it,
But also the white ice
Of so much fever broken like plowed earth,
The shore that breaches shore.
It makes you Lady of this place
Naked Umbel that the wind bears
Silent with braziers our beauty.

Then, so beautiful, the sea bears her away.

III

I see you deserted peopled
But always expanse of seas
For you are opal

Winter had this substance
Of hands that burgeon in dark
Summer, country soon ruined.

Between his hands he keeps it
Like a strange head of hair
And it is a pity to lie upon it.

IV

There, upon the clay of stones
Memory has deposited
Like a shipwreck reddish with pinks
Like an ossuary of loves.

But where are the fields that come undone?
Where go the fields when winter dawns?
So many seas have crossed us.

V

In me you are mountain
Country O impure visage
Of a pure visage shattered.
The storm built these ramparts
The sea that you haunt burns
I see no birds that are not frightened.
Do you think the storm lies?
These ramparts have surrounded us.

VI

Its good fortune had so ripened
That the river was cold and pure
The love of wandering is a childish love.

Star, this is the fountain
Where you die on a good day!
A tree's faith neither dies nor lasts.

VII

Then you were tillage fallen
From havoc of mad horses
Were you plain that measures
The mountain's pasturage
Which it makes into its howling wolves?

Leave evil to the shipwrecked
Wind of sand is wind of torture,
Our joy is born just after.

VIII

Tillage, O country, pure visage
Of a visage impure and wounded.
The wind makes merry in the bird
The storm has left you behind
Here commences the breakage.

And gather the storm from the organ
It transmutes within you and has no end
until this murmur is no longer night.

Promenade of Solitary Death

The sad bay has not moved
On a lake of roses, strewn
With pale bodies in the rosebushes
Funereal bay it has remained

The shore hesitates the sea passes
The boats are water scourers
Black is the sand, the color
Is evident in this place

The birds here cloak the murky sky
with the gray of their takeoffs
Such evidence has rendered mad
The first wave run aground

Waves from madness to madness
Pale and wan the others have followed
The rosebushes have kept the alms
Of suicides upon their surplice

The white race of frigate birds
Never comes to these repasts
They go to sound other death knells
Where the wind wears no gloves

Here there move only the flutter
Of memory and this high cry
That was heard one August noon
On the cliff and its flock

A cry of earth that deploys
The nervures of its foliage
Because love shall have searched it
Or because the rain is pleasing

A cry of woman torn open
At the edge of the fallows
Her nubile breasts divided
Between misery and moss

Cry of deadbolt and cry of osprey
And this people was asleep
The bird of prey makes its nest
Upon the living ash of the tree

And there still moves only milk
Of seaweeds this smell,
Death vivifies death
Funereal bay it has remained

But sad it has not moved
Upon its lake of hatreds, strewn
With pale bodies in the thickets
Who pardon you, O rosebushes.

NOTE

frigate bird: A formerly common bird that has become extremely scarce in the French
Antilles.

The Book of Offerings

Reanimated in this secret
I know you to be the bank
That was kindled upon their love
By imperceptible lookouts

They were passing through obscure places
Where the word is divined
And where hands take root
Between the secular signs

O sprightly one, mute tillage
You were hieratic stem
Victim or bud of tempests
I know you mysterious being

Desire infancy of morning
The knotted cry the knotted blood
Unknotted blood of our pains
And its infancy without desire

I know you to be the infancy
Yet there, I know you
To have grown up, mute oak
Upon the ambiguity of your stones

Terrified to be upon the water
Like a solemn crowd
Disendraped upon your altars
They shall have completely encircled you

Upon the singular love of banks
You scatter your body
In vain: the storm is already dead
All is serious without consanguinity

Oh this place is lists of outrages
The briar blooms lowly there
Loves there live on ruins
I know you dungeons of waters

Immobile and immured earth
In your silence, fragile
There is but one place for truth
Which takes pain, O doleful one

There is but one place which for prop
Chooses man from the hills
Fills him with ardent victims
Teaches him cruelty

Where is the much vaunted singular one?
This people dies, are you its silence
Eternity of storms divined
Upon suffering

Splendor O fleeting reason
Splash sole gift
Waves which are the opening
And vigil of bodies without care

All is naked, rich, save with enticements
Toward the mass of lands I toil
Oh I abandon the tides
—Knowing you to be mystery

And water's edge, when all is extinguished.

THE RETURN TO THE SEA

for Cécile Moinault

The House of Sands

I

Summer, fleeting grace in this water's edge are hidden.
Patient ones, here it is that you wander free of time
Lovers of yourselves left to yourselves
Women, lichens lost when you pass through.

In this love which sheds its vestments of worn-out dawns
O strand, upon which the mornings are crimes!
Sands, which blew away your shores toward the summits,
And kites, remembrances of yesterday hurled into the sky!

II

Country, when the rains take hold in the sun,
Where the smithies of water braze a rainbow
Man projects, after the storm, upon the Salt
His taciturn shadow and his noiseless hope.

Silence had fled the ardent solitude
Triumphal Palms! The deserted day swept upon the flowers;
Ever in between fear and desire, hesitates
The wounded love that shall strew the day.

O night, country of carnage of opprobrium,
Of larvae that endlessly foretell their future
To the skies where sleeps the sempiternal bird.

III

Ships you wander in immobility
Alone you retain corroded water on your loins,
Place upon the water's edge where the gaze is confirmed.

Do you fear the dawn that gleaned the stormfields
Drowned tired at the shroud of the first voice,
To drink the water that grazes on the dawn of seashores
And the earth buried in you too late?

Death beauty glory eternity! toils
Of the sower in glittering space, for whom
The Salt comes to pain and is always erased.

IV

As at last the word invokes your absence
You are sea, like an infanta, also like
Woman, washing the salt in nocturnal cabins.

Sea manifested, watched by buried gardens
Your face uproots its bird,
Higher than clouds wastes the wheat of seas.

Orchards, glaciers, impure clay that ferments
Beneath the foam see this day in which I see you
Visage turned into disinherited tillage.

Oh the ocean so calm, and calm, this undergrowth!
The day brings Passover, its lover, to grief there.
There the sun reposes in gentle cruelties.

Verses

I

Who sees death, he does not know the pepper trees setting with gold
This high book of summits where the river lays out its goods, nor,
O mystery
Upon the sand the cocks, unexpected sleepers.

This is the azure sand strewn with black sand, it was the tear
That we buried yesterday on the bank, near the dead sails.
And the gum trees, dreams of wind, of living sails,

Scarcely decorate the mute wound of rocks! All this was up there
The solitude, then a sheep whose throat was cut as a festal offering,
Weaving the dregs of its death, when day comes.

II

And the poet knows himself, but still before him the fullness of time,
Of tempests: this is a sea that summons itself, and finds itself not.
As a jealous sea, itself its own lover, rends itself,
Wild with fury—up to the trees, which it cannot reach.

III

I embraced the sand, I waited between the rocks, I kissed
The water then the sand, the rocks—this heart of rough things—then
a tree! Crying out
That language come undone and thus bathe, in this place,
Whoever would have shed light upon the mirage, and made it purer.
—The three nettles of ignorance have grown before my door!

What is this place, what is this tree on the cliff,
What never stops falling?

IV

You raised your corolla, asked the day for its swarm of pale eyes,
where the river strains and the storms took hold.

Oh! undoing the day he brings to light peoples, loves—but what river are we talking about if not the storm, in which this image shall have bathed?

And so, wave of wave, your own endless seashore, are you real from the sea or still shore of this dream?

(And this, coming down from the tree, is the same cliff, the rocks, this heart of sands, this sea!)

V

Pollens, snowing trees, snowy sowings!
Groan the memory of your saps in the ground
And the softened forehead of your quarrels in the wind.

Already winter, already, and again this silence.
A long silent voyage without the red water ever reviving us
A pure going a pure shorebank and an apse no less pure
As from a fabulous India that dwindles away, suddenly human,
And comes to die in the mirror of your death.

VI

I see this country as imaginary only because suffering,
And on the contrary, quite real, this is suffering before joy,
Seafroths!—barely there, they take fright and die. As we see:
"Upon the gravels, astonished with saltings,
A people walks within the tempest of its name!
And the fireflies accompany it."

VII

Still, and unknown, in whom the night marries its dawn,
   There is no joy but that which is serene, beside the dead sands, there
is no mirror but your bodies,
   In which the wave of time denudes its season! The one
   Who goes forth knotting his word with seafroths and gambols upon
the mirror of the sand—still he dies.
   The seafroth knows neither pain nor time.

VIII

Sand, savor of solitude! when we pass into it forever.
O night! more than the path struck with twilights, alone.
In the infinity of sand its rout, in the valley of night its rout and yet
upon the salt,
There are only calyxes, encompassing the stem-posts of these seas,
where delight is infinite to me.

And what to say of the Ocean, except that it waits?

IX

By the holy rape of imperfect light upon light to be perfected,
By the unknown, gentleness forcing gentleness to open itself,
You are love that passes beside me, O village of depths,
But your water is thicker than my leaves will ever be heavy.

And what to say of the Ocean, except that it waits?

X

Toward the infinite flesh, is this waiting broken at the root, an
evening of hail?
Oh! to be farther from you than for example air from root, I have no
longer leaf or sap.
But I go back up into the fields and the storms which are roads of the
country of knowledge,
Pure in the air of myself, and embolden myself with oblivion if the
hail comes.

(And what to say of the Ocean, except that it waits?)

Consecration

Delicious dangerous approach of noon. The tree's shadow is vertigo of naked soul which within itself consults and decides. Then, the blind victories. These ways of seawrack born from branch, which sway in the breeze, being mistaken. They believe in the wave, it is the wind.

Youthful phantasms, unhoped-for nests of silence!

THE INDIES

for Pierre Reynal

THE CALL

1492. The Great Discoverers hurl themselves upon the Atlantic, in search of the Indies. With them begins the poem. Also all those, before and after this New Day, who have known their dream, lived off it or died from it. The imagination creates ever new Indies, for which men quarrel with the world. Those who left Spain and Portugal, lusting after gold and spices; but soldiers and mystics too. The Poem names Father Labat, Jacobin and corsair; then the Negro prophet whom he had whipped bloody, the one who had seen the boats burgeon on the sea, before they appeared; and names Toussaint-Louverture, slave and liberator of Haiti . . . but we must not get ahead of history: here, the port is on holiday, the adventure coalesces; the dream is exhausted by its own project. Man fears his desire at the moment of satisfying it.

I

Upon Genoa the field of adventure-bells shall open.
O lyre of bronze and wind, in the lyrical air of departures,
The anchor is in order! . . . And sweet stupefaction,
Let us be done with! in the distance of another salting.
Oh the seasalt is more propitious here than the bishop's holy water,
Meanwhile the crowd is silent; and it hears the sequence of history . . .
City, listen! and be pious! Religion be accomplished for you in our
  hearts,
Who have known the thrill and the compass, and other works under sail.

II

The man stops his gesture, and says, holding the scum: "This combat
Was of scum, of faith, of suns and blood,
In which gold, stained with blood, played its essential part, and
  madness also!"
And someone says: "We are a beach for scum, O son."
He says . . . We, on the beach, are given leave to assemble at the
  prow of the voice, to cry out
On the beach, Lightning, the only reason of those who scour the sea.

III

He says; and the beach knows not, at this beginning, from which
    foam shall be made
Anointment or havoc? No one knows, bare feet on the bare table,
Of which Indies this marks approach and praise, or which this captain
(Blinded by winds or diamonds?)
That the voice on the beach yet summons to depart, loosing the
    mooring shackle?
—But this science is more profound.

IV

Like the Negro in the mountains who predicted
The imminent passage of a shipload of new women and saucepans
(Women from New Rochelle and saucepans of white-iron, he said),
And suffered brine and pepper at the hands of a priest—skinned alive!
But didn't the ship come into dock, caressing with its moist canvas
The country of tough meat and death!

V

It is not yet time. However the night of faith, or the same night, of
    depths,
Is already turning into seasalt, and not, cleric's accomplices, dirty
    brines
That inebriate the flesh and hurl the crazed soul to the top of the
    masts, O pain!
Toward the top, toward the sand, through this ocean, so high!
As though to tear from each wound the thick maize of the unknown.

VI

Indies! it was thus, by your name nailed upon madness, that the sea
    began.
Tell me, Had it taken form or birth before that day
When the old men from that quarter that the sun turned green got up
And said, stammering: "Whither goes the wind, there are the Indies!"?
They prayed. And made their god into a staff to plant on the first shoal.
Then they left.

VII

What was the sea, and its scum? Could they know its promise was not
    expiring in some abyss far from all the known routes?
For a long time the voice of man was thus lost in the temples
As obscure as the way to the temple was! And this sea,
Did they not think it would flow into infinity, a gaping glutton, till it
    was dry?
Then they hailed the opposite bank!

VIII

Each one saw that the ocean was in commerce with itself, on the
    other shore of life.
That it was rich in mango trees, silks, spices, narrow streets
(But where was the spice, and where the silk, you ask now?)
And each one cried out that the ocean is a hard force, which is tested,
    found impure,
And feeds off its own flesh!

IX

Like that Negro we were talking about, who was tortured.
In his cask of fulminations, he kept the language of prophecy.
Forgetful of your pepper, Labat, and the three times one hundred
    spouts of the sacrificial whip! he said
As the women opened their women's eyes on this still-virgin sun . . .
And wasn't it brine, the bolt of the soul, that seized him on the
    Mount of his passion
Upon the sea that he saw grow out of a single life? The sea O sage!
Through which the folly of man, and his pillage, and his beauty,
    begin to be known.

X

So in Sparta was Terpandrius punished, who had found his lyre too light
(And added two strings to it).
In Verona two died, whose bread was love, whose clothing was the
    night.
And Toussaint! who held a lyre of flames and entrails, he

Was thrown into the white sea of the Jura; where provoked by snow, sarcasm,
And hunger, he was finally able to die, so rigid, in his armchair.
They all knew the sea, barely or well, and their unequal brine unites them.
The Indies are eternity.

XI

They call out to each other, wonderful, and become acquainted on the beach where Time invites them;
On the same sand each time, their feet having traced the glory of the tides;
Rocks on the sea, unknown to those who live on higher ground, but breaking seas and carving towns!
In them Time gorges itself with Songs, and the seawrack stirred not its fragile cry,
Torrent where is drawn which Indies?

XII

I had drunk; I had drunk that water, because it was blue, and I knew
The beginning of paths among the brambles, the thorns, the red mud and the bulls;
Pale with that ash beneath the salt (as in Carthage when it was destroyed!
As, concealed in the salt of distance, from the Gold Coast to Maracaibo,
Ash of ship's hold and the storeroom's cane syrup!) I had known the approach of that water.

XIII

So did I see them come down between the thornbushes and the bulls;
The solitary ones, who died on that path of rabble, called the Path of Silk;
The proud, coiffed with lances, who named the sea their soul's accomplice;
The horse trainer in a long robe, who taught his men sixty languages;
The new gun, the dark diamonds of the latecomers; who were no less drunk!

XIV

Oh no one knows where the moon-watcher, orient, comes from;
Nor the west? The west is a lake, moon-pasture in which other
    nascent sky-eaters
Mix with those who eat injustices and crimes.
For who, upon the tempest of the shore, could tell wise man from
    victim?

XV

How many are there, that I counted but who went to drink
At the fountain of their own voices, where henceforth there is great
    music.
And they tried to exhort me, but I did not take shape with their seas,
And now I listen, from afar I violate the vigor of this time.
Welcome me, O fountain-makers at the edge of the sand, who for so
    long was so lacking in wisdom.

XVI

Great love, splendid night's work, or humblest dove,
This night I wish they should delight in yet another flight
Of words and treachery on scum and ardor.
Love is dead.
Oh no one knows where it lies, dove grown weary of words, the secret
Of raw love, of millet and wisdom, but the word is not mute any
    more!
Many were they who spoke thus.

XVII

So on all sides, there was and is harvest of couples, each thing
Sheathing in its black heart the contrary soul of its song, and each tear
Signing nearby the coal that sweated it, and every faith washing off its
    crime,
And each voice keeping its rhyme for the *Land*-ho! of the lookouts,
    and every sea
Bathing its sea on the other side! All confusion and vigor!

And the sailor says he even thinks, children, that there are two Indies,
    two leavenings of bloody gold!
But the Indies are truth.

XVIII

How many are there, who call to each other on the beach, men of
    history, near wide-open Genoa?
Bells! Clamor of girls on their way to the port, with fiancés aboard.
Drunkenness of one (is it not the doctor?) sick to be there, who
    searches the horizon, saying "How far, how far?"
And then the cables, quick, the rigging, everything singing and crying
    out, the girls laughing, cannons, prayers! . . .
And the silence, enormous in a new sea, which opens
The Two Books of bloody azure blue.

THE VOYAGE

The Fear. During the three months (an eternity) that they floated on the infinity of the ocean, the sailors became acquainted with ambiguity; they learned that the North, asylum of the compass-needle, is duplicitous. What did they not suffer? A man on the sea pays tribute to his secular bonds, to his tranquil establishment. Fear ennobles what is venal, and peoples the sea with sparkling cathedrals. It is ascesis. What began as a mere shadow between Home and Knowledge, it makes worthy of a new sand: the inexhaustible Voyage. "In three days," Columbus finally told them, "I shall give you a world." On the twelfth of October, 1492, the anchor was thrown, within sight of the forests, under a blazing sun.

XIX

Voyage, muffled voyage, when the storms had their part, and madness.
The star considers; it is silence, it cannot do what it would like.
The frigate bird, floating in the winds, greets it with a round of
    waves, and turns blue,
Or the frigate on the water, summit of this wake that no wave betrays!
Voyage! a world of biscuits, bets, wretchedness. Where it is always
    midnight,
For the hours cannot escape.

XX

Far back behind, escape! O peaceful vacuity of stone benches,
    anointed by the centuries!
Mother! Mother-of-pearl of those the autumn had shod, village
    women of desire!
So tender in their skirts when the fires of Saint John fulfilled their
    vigil.
The man steps back beneath the sail, he flees the wind; he sees the
    past, warmer,
That calls to him, that murmurs, more secretly than that dead flame,
Or than this woman's body where the flame is now.

XXI

"Tack to the stern! Clew up the sail of the future! Let us drink fresh
water and throw into the sea,
With the fresh water those who wish to see where the Gods go. Let us
fear the impure scurvy,
Bolt of the Invisible that we insult. Break the trunks. Overboard, the
provisions!
What are they to us, these Indies where no one knows if the grass
grows for our mouths,
For our thirst, our pleasure, in this moment already of great thirst for
wine!"
But who, seamen, can avoid the Indies?

XXII

Green Goddesses, I hear you on this voyage, after the twenty-third
night.
More silent than the star, you nailed them, these male midwives of
stars, you!
Arena to muffled sharks, the sea is the tournament field.
There they hurl themselves, arms hacking top and sou'westers, the
two heroes!
Land's Past, recumbent in its tepid night,
And Chaos! the courted dawn of every land.

XXIII

O Geysers . . . the morning waits not for tomorrow, which it accosts,
at the sad dawn,
Nor for evening, when the phosphors of the sea shall write their
limits.
But it waits for the end, it is the ship's boy of hope, all day long,
It says, "Pass, time, with the passing of time I grow larger"; then it is
afraid!
And this is a sound of madness, of very ancient history in its head.
And a sound of gold and battles in its heart.

XXIV

Time passes, that has no time left save that of buckets and rigging,
of hard wind.
Unknown Middle Ages whose voice is beneath the waves, and the
hopeless mastage.
O Time of the Auto-da-Fé or of the Stout Burg where Frankish words
were enmasted.
With the ship's boys on deck, who are serfs at mercy.
With its duke, umbrageous captain, who each day from his battlement,
to reassure the sailors,
Makes the gesture of saluting toward the west!

XXV

He who, panting, touches the past in every fiber, and reveres it,
Who with gentle tears mourns his youth and his parents, he likes to
drink
From the glass of oblivion the sudden venom of sweet familiar things;
This one makes his feverish time on the sea into wisdom, provided he
goes on unsealing the wave!
And concedes by his name the rising wave to the wave of the past.

XXVI

Time passes, when man is the ship's boy of hope and the gear treats
him badly.
Time passes, in which language cries out its flight, upon this cirque
where there is no mountain and no echo.
From sunrise to sunset, the same weight of words, which are birds of
such silence, fallen.
From one side to the other the bother of measuring that thickness,
and all this noise,
So that, on the gravel whence a path of gold goes off down there
toward other seas,
Language should know the gold of impious gods!

XXVII

Evening: moment of moon, and memory, and imagery.
The eager horde has come to know distress and the science of white
    days. The water burns, O moon, upon hope.
The wave turns! Where does it lead? Of what fruits does it hold the
    bitter sweat?
This desire in the human heart, where does it lead, already so blue,
Between the one land, and the other?

XXVIII

Time passes, in which hermits made their home, who are nomads on
    the sea.
One of the nomads was laid to rest this day, upon the oblique plank
    (which one is it?)
Tied with a rag from his trunk: a Flemish sheet, with an embroidered
    heart
Souvenir more than sheet, for he slept in that hammock . . . After the
    amen, he slipped away
Toward that other solitude, halfway, or near the banks, who can say?
The green water woos and delivers him from this knot.

XXIX

He, the silent one who belonged to the sand of absence, and wished
    to leave
A memory to the volcanoes and the suns and the splendors of the
    past,
Weep, oh mourn him, goddesses who sleep when the wind thrusts,
On the untouched sand of your beds, where now he lies alone,
And sing him your bodies! A half-flight from his language, your lover.

XXX

He will not know if time has taken shape in a new, or more secret
    realm?
(Awakening forests or burning altars?)
If that flame he dreamed of bore the name of maturity? nor whether
    the Indies,

Indies for his pleasure or his madness or his cupidity, are down there, really

Indies? He shall never know (mourned by you!)

Never, the end of this journey! nor the last word with the boat on the sand that glides, and then the kneeling man who embraces his utterance.

Time passes. Passes.

XXXI

O Geysers . . . The wanderer does not know the quay of rotten wood (Like the one who has sea in the river or the lake of his childhood,

Peaceful in his waiting for the port of call; and who unfolds, the night before, his costume; then buckles the straps!)

The hermit does not expect the Land to emerge from its well without surprise at the appointed hour of dawn.

No. One day at noon, it will come! At the moment of greatest terror it will come, announced by birds!

Or perhaps they will discover it one morning, but already so close to the topsail

That the useless cry of the sentinel will scintillate from tree to tree,

All the way to the springs that are visible, up there!

XXXII

Land! Tempests vanquished! You unavowed gods! O Prayer of Seas!

Middle Ages, Desert, fertilized! O Parabolas of vines and wheatfields! Tears of the Past!

They have met the land, and step back into their history to consider it!

They assemble on this beach, the virgin beach where is no mooring.

They will start a market: of men and of gods—but the language ripens within them!—

Of spices, gold, and yellow fever!

THE CONQUEST

These conquerors lusted to death after the gold and silver mines of the New World. They vanquished the banks, then the forest, then the Andes, then the High Plains with their deserted cities. They sacked the very space, in their covetous and insanely mystical fury. Tragic Song of love for the New World. Progressive exaltation, massacre, and final solitude. A rupture is consummated; but man does not give up the dream. He will repopulate what he has depopulated. Pillage shall be followed by pillage. The various names of the Conqueror: Cortez, Pizarro, Almagro, Balboa. The insane assassin: Father Valverde. The one he baptized before strangling: Atahualpa, last lover of the red earth.

XXXIII

Each vessel seduces her silent bay; mystery of sand.

"Sound the charge! Strike the water! Clamors, deforest the virgin
   solitude!

The Forest, on the Palankeen of its warmth, will swaddle us in loves,
   and by cool drinks cure us!"

Love! O naked beauty! where are the sentinels? Here appear the lovers.

To allocate the virgin's gold, they have a scale; and to kill, they are
   weighers of lightning.

Their language shall be virile to you, O earth, O dazzled woman,
   your red blood mixed with your red clay.

They, thick with their beards! but thicker still the word of the captain!

The step of his horse and the machete's spurt are the words of his
   hymnal.

He advances, he is a mirage, O sacred depths of mines full of gold
   and silver!

From bays to forests, in the sky, then in the cities, you hear the proud
   thunder.

He marches, the oracle announces him; he woos you. And his love
   crucifies you.

XXXIV

Saying:
"Are you a fairy, whose gems I have known, and whose smile was the
  wind?
Are you this flame, outwardly peaceful, in which the wind held its
  wedding?
Are you this desire, more desirable than the woman of dawn, naked?
Are you, in this poem of myself who implore you, the poem of
  yourself, finally come?
O virgin! your lovers I shall kill with only modicum of rage; with care.
They adorn themselves with the gold of your breasts, and these jewels
  set fire to me!
I shall melt the gold, the part of you that I reserve for my kiss,
O virgin! here is the alchemist of your body, soldier of faith,
And who loves you in a great wind of madness and blood, he is in you!
Come onto the bank of your soul! Hold out your treasures for your
  conquistadors!"
But the bank dozed in its eternity.

XXXV

Saying:
"I implore you, I who have come from elsewhere and from my
  dreams, I keep watch.
Your hair, in its thickness, keeps the stirring of my eternity; I am
  foundering,
My nose bleeds (weeping with desire) as I climb toward you.
Do not be mysterious, to the point of hiding the wonders of your body
I want to descend as far into you as life can permit.
Do not betray, you, this old desire, older than the boldness of the old
  world!
Ah! my body is stretched toward the height of your beauties, I am
  climbing now,
Condor of your mountains; I adore the serpent, your holy son!
In the linen of your forests I lose my fingers, I cut and shape the linen;
Do not be silent, do not be clothed thus, I am still trembling!"
But the forest rustled and soughed in its eternity.

XXXVI

Saying:
"These men, sons of bitches, who knew you before me!
From what divine voice did they receive the message to adore you?
    Which god was it,
Or which archangel gave them license to stretch out upon the
    beautiful?
Do they know the joy of evening, when the vine gleams with yellow
    fervor?
Have they a tender lover's language that caresses gently with words?
Have they the face of a fearsome lover, who has removed neither
    breastplate nor boots?
Do they know the one and the other face of things, the two earths?
Come, come! I burn and am bright with burning; volcano
Scattered upon the uncalmed volcanoes of your altitudes, which, like
    me, are at the point of dying!
These men, in order to possess you, I shall kill them, to the last one!
    It is done, here is their blood."
And the mountain trembled in its eternity.

XXXVII

Saying:
"My god is the only god, my desire the only desire!
They have given me to you, and you to me in a dawn of combats,
Of flesh and lust and new divinities! I am descending, crowned with
    azure, straight in the saddle,
Toward the valley where are cities that fasten your adornments, dead
    cities!
Here they are, deserted! Oh to people them with flame, in which the
    silver melts!
And if a man comes, an old man who knew you long before me,
May he be baptized and then strangled! so that the soul should be
    saved
While the body rots in you, but far from you! (I court you, dirty
    cavalier,

I! whose blood was lava) . . . And if he refuse the water that cleanses
us of this sin, there on his forehead,
Then raise, amid the gold, raise the just flame of a pyre; burn him!"
But the gentle city wept in its eternity.

XXXVIII

Love, stubborn love of pools lapped by ethereal tongues, where the
chapel of lianas
In the air that rises and blooms composes a face, tenderly.
Where is the woman, springtime? Where is her soul, torn by the lover
And the laughing and sobbing of the man drunk on a purer water,
And the gold of her hands washed in the fountain of lianas, where the
coyotes weep?
Stubborn, the urn of the freshly chosen one (after the humble
perfume of the one abandoned),
More out of reach each time, woman of banks, woman of brush,
woman
Of red lands, of volcanoes; and then on the Plateau where we go
down, woman of cities!
More out of reach, and this is desire, the same always, of flesh that
will not yield, adept
In its horizon, knotted body . . . Oh the horizon never dies, is never
Capsized by the stars that are desire's undoing! . . . —And the horse
advances, and the cavalier cries out.

XXXIX

Saying:
"No more laughing! I cry out your unpinnate sex where there are
mines of cool metal.
So beautiful, you were my dream, and here you are; there is no longer
any temple to hide the star.
Undo the front of your lair! Undo the horizon's venom, undo.
By Pizarro and by Cortez! By all the bellies of the sky! And by the
sword!
No leaf left unmarked by the muskets' seal!
No rock left unweighed by our scale! This is justice.

And if the Indies are not here where you lie down, what difference is
    it to me?
Indies, I shall put you into words. West Indies: to restore my dream.
So that nothing should be lost, of this wild vision. It is a good
    picture; I shall keep it.
Get up now, we shall load the heavy vessels."
The woman was silent, so beautiful, in her eternity.

XL

Saying:
"Back, thing impure in your limpidness! On your knees, incorporeal
    woman!
Come, in my hand which is at once soldier's and priest's I shall give
    you,
The air of depths to drink, the water of sky to eat, with its fish!
Stop! Cover up your nakedness, that I may see you, red hostess.
Pick the roughest cloth, lofty perfumes, and do not forget raw gold!
The hair of your sky, to which this star led me, I make the braid of it
Innumerable, and our conjugal bed . . . The summer takes us, opens us,
You, liquid; I made of fever. Where is the mine, where are the
    chariots, and the spasms?
Bitch! I shall burn noon on your belly, and slaughter
Every ewe in every cabin, and rape your soft night's child for this
    dream!"
But the earth, so naked, kept the vow of its eternity.

XLI

Love, stubborn law, azure nave, and old threatened eagle's dream.
O mystery, smoke rises from the victims, and their arms are sheathed
    by dark blood.
In the absolute air, desire marks the inviolate genital's location, where
    are the mines.
Horses amble past, and their nostrils search the soil, keeping watch
    over the spot.
There is no city or azure on which the god's gaze has not left its mark!
Man is this god when he kills a man, or humiliates him with holy
    water; when he weighs.

He is this eagle on the woman, and this woman suits him, he melts
   on the goddess.
He spreads her on the silver altar, enriched with gold, but this god
   trembles. O terrors!
Again the day embellishes the poem of loving, for the denuded
   maiden, the red one.
The assault recommences, in a fog propitious to such love, a fog of
   blood!
Then, one evening, the horse shakes night, and beholds the sky
   without any eagle!—Man is alone.
Ah! Only he remains in his love which is so red.

XLII

Saying:
"You deceived me, woman of this west! O inebriations! O torrents!
What may he drink now, the lover come from afar, what ardor, O
   moon?
I know the savage love that depopulates and uproots itself; it is mine!
So much sweat and ocean, to arrive at such desolation! Oh I shall
   stay!
And I shall rip to pieces your dung of jaguars and serpents! I, who
   entered through the Gate of the Sun!
I know a people down there in whom I shall trade; whom I shall
   hook up to your tit.
For your lovers whom I killed, stubborn love leads me to where are
   the heavy, crawling fish.
A people, O woman, who shall have you all night long for their
   pleasure and their pain.
At dawn, I shall scratch the black rind and make fall the secret dew.
So that my desire may assume durable form! So that the morning may
   belong to me, and the moon too!"
Now the earth wept, knowing what eternity is.

THE TRADE

The slave trade. Which shall never be erased from the face of the sea. On the west coast of Africa, the flesh merchants receive their stock. During two centuries the rich traffic more or less openly supplies the Islands, North America, and in no lesser proportion, Central and South America. Here a massacre (in the reservoir of Africa) is enacted, in order to compensate for the massacre over there. Monstrous mobilization, oblique crossing, Poem of Death. A language of unreason, but which carries a new reason. For it is also the beginning of a Unity, the other part of an agreement finally commuted. This is the Indies of suffering, after the Indies of dream. Now reality is daughter of man truly: born of the contradictions he has lived and brought about.

XLIII

Lord of the poem where Shadow shall reign, Sun! You weep the splendor of this place, when you set fire to the other face of your power. Your course is immense, O immobile one; upon your city of splendor dreams the night, your wife. You devastate the here and now with your wife's cry of joy; then down there you beget the morning, the swallow of light. Ancient. To so many courses dedicated, getting caught in your own snare, do you not await the harbor? Where are your Indies? Where your light? Are you the heart of a man carted hither and yon? Heart of a man burned, that he might recollect such fire? After the seashore studded with glory, after the time when out of the desert arose thirst and an instability that is excessively measured, also after the torrid love of the sex of profusion, such a rare love! soon there opens an ocean of narrow, dark things among those piled up in the dank hold and led to your west, to die there in you, broker of stolen goods.

XLIV

Horrors and hard prose . . . These were, in the morning, open Indies of epic, of a body flatulent with ambition. These were, didn't you know, solitary Indies, where the dream turned its spindle toward the tranquil past: but on the ocean, man recoils. Of fires and soldiers (with shoulders of dejected women, all the way to the tired Cities), these were Indies of triumphal march, on the marble road. What soldier would know how to narrate the flavor of that road? And these will be, we may say, milky Indies, whose wandering soul is perfumed in enclosed gardens. Melted into this ruby of poem, distinct Indies, to your east and west, voyager! . . . The raw word, without elegance or happiness. Man is miserly with his tears, and the shadow is among him . . . These are the Indies, for today, of unreason; earths, without place and without orient, of rape and of suicide—for those who do not wish to see the terrible bed of your night.

XLV

You passed over their desires, without them seeing you: they with whom the enormous Indies of misfortune would be populated. Through the cupola of the forest, to them your filtered love was sweet and without furor. They knew not the thick obverse of your triumphs: their night had no peer. By mouth they venerate the fire that is spat out on the altar. Men of night, these were suns of black blood; their princes wooed the earth, in which each people had sealed its shore, its path. O solitary warrior! They had war of their gods and of their hunger . . . This evening, around the torches, the euphoria of the women mourns the dead lord, the red-eyed lord. In the palace, servants and wise men are silent; a child widens to excess the eye of his solitude. Smoke, pale now, bends toward the multicolored god, and it is a good sign: tomorrow there will be a man upon the wooden iguana, to receive the crowd . . . You passed, only visible through the soaring vault, like a post quivering with spears.

XLVI

I know, I who address you, O star, that they were bloody and naked! They found joy on the road, like a rock: picked up and thrown away, that a rustle of branches might stir someone. They also knew the avenues of the plain, the solstices. Their streets, in the open, followed the river of your fires. Their capitals studded other forests, but whose roofs were of azure. And they annotated with great ease the work of those who inebriated the universe . . . I do not say, I who speak to you: behold the great ones of the past. I do not say that they were alone, or that the altar belonged to them. Nonetheless, I plunge into the very flame through which you laugh. I go back up the street of your eternity, until that night of their suffering. Naked, terrible when the tigers advanced. Did they not drift along the river of your tears, down that way? One of them deported from East to West, for which Indies, do you know? Bloody and naked, of burned blood, lunatic nakedness: and all the while, the sea says nothing.

XLVII

The Wise Man squats, solemn. "Do not trust the one whose Poem is debased and whose Word turns hard, just because he suffers his word. May he be deprived of the use of his voice, may his hands be fettered, may he meditate. If he would be reborn into the splendor he has tried to say, untie his arms, ungag him. Otherwise, let him rot in his stiflement, in his excess!" Then the wise man goes away, silent, dreaming of heavy drapings of glaciers . . . The sentenced man dries up in the room, the ship's hold, desperate amid the odor of the sea. All night long, through the porthole, he sees the waves pass by. They carry the day after into the brambles of the day before. And the word is more circuitous and sterile, if possible . . . Crossing, night of ice. Who dreams of splendor? Who has dreamed of an island of perfume and sweet cinnamon? Man accomplishes his ocean; he berates his sea. And he smothers, it is true.

XLVIII

How many times, how many days will you offer yourself, abyss, to the patience of the migrating herd? . . . The lover returning, sweeter each time and more obscure, does she know, in the voice of him who awaits her, this nuance of fallacy? Just as you appear to your servants, does she know the appearance of green water in the heart of the one who awaits her? And this other (or is it the same?) who is laughed at in the square, and who accepts derision; the wind does not know if she is loved. But that she is whipped with nettles when her lover fears the clarity of her gaze, and that shoals are complicitous with fear, the wind tells us this! . . .Thus fearful of the little salting the mark of your dream would inflict on their skin, at this point you bestir yourself, you ocean, at this point you muss your hair, you give yourself dizzily to the word of this wind, that those whom you fear and who endure you each day can see neither rigging nor sails; so they should die in the hold, amid the odor of cramped-up death. While so near them and so far away, you simulate the anger in which loves expire.

XLIX

A people has been shut up in ships of the line, flesh has been sold, rented, bartered. And the old ones for menial tasks, men to the harvest of sugar, and the woman for the price of her child. No longer any mystery or audacity: the Indies are the market of death; the wind shouts it now aloud, directly on the prow! Those who have burned love and desire; these are Navigators. They have turned their faces toward the forest; dumb, they ask for some word. Language, another time, of nudity. For muscle, so many words. O deserted Language, and its mortuary grammar! For a set of teeth, so many more . . . Up to the Omega of the new world! Now, very long ago, I see Cyrus leading his people to the watering hole, at the hour when you become red with another hope, sun. Cyrus, betrayed master who flogs, then insults you, sea. Have you forgotten the watering place of pain and the whip of light? I see a raw sun and a sea of wearinesses, which support on this blood the great Indies with no mystery.

L

"One of them, taking advantage of the chain gangs' inadvertence, turned his soul toward the sea and was engulfed. Another degenerate whose body is prairieless, riverless, fireless. One who expires in his dung consumed in the common fetidness. One here who knows his wife is chained up near him: he does not see her, but he hears her weakening. And One who knows his wife tied up over there to the wood of a slave ship: he does not see her but he hears her leave. Yet another whose club has broken some rib, but the sailor so wanton with booty is punished. And One who is led onto the deck once a week, so that his legs do not rot. One who will not walk, already immobile in his death, who is made to dance on the sheet-iron of fire. One who awaits death from starvation, refuses to swallow the bread moistened with salt; but he is offered the choice of this bread or red-hot iron from the fire. One who finally swallows his tongue, and smothers, motionless in his red slobber. There is a scientific name for it which I cannot recall, but which is known to the depths of the sea since that time, without any doubt."

LI

A child climbs to the highest point of the earth, and upon the horizon sees the cargo burgeon: "It's a new one! arriving for the Lenten market!" Then he blows into the conch's throat, and the vendors down below ready themselves for the acquisition of young girls and males . . . Where is the flame, where the splendor in this new Dividing of the world? The acquisitor rises; at his belt is the list that he shall haggle over. I have drawn up the list, the hard stanza, of those who were upon the ocean of death, and here is what I am told: "Churl's list, beyond measure! . . . Old story, without any leavening! Word and poem, with neither depth nor shadow" . . . Let's get started! the auctioneers strut on the platforms, they parcel out life; the merchants hurry; the sweet child slips to the bottom of the path, giving up the space of annunciation. He does not know, adolescent watcher of the future, that there will be other auctions for the misfortune of prophecies; that there will be some, of furious heels upon the drum of night, and whose drunkenness will speak: "We are sons of those who survived."

LII

O Sun! O ancient work deafly mingled with sea, and of love's hue. Every morning one man opens his eyes upon the solitude in which he keeps himself. He has quit flamboyancies, wept over dreams, abandoned the rare blueness of those who love and are loved. He looks, he stirs himself, the day is dense with rumors; what shall he not have to budge in this knot of indivisible onslaughts, out of which sense must be made. After the crossing, the solitude, and the anger of the sharks, there soon opens a field of sumptuous lands, of poverty and fires, and of hurled black blood. It is of the race of ripe things to ripen in heavy fire and tumultuous encumbrance. We have taken a step on hard earth, and each one now struggles to distinguish his pure West from this East; there has never been a question of any other course; O Sun, and you Sea, we shall know your metrics and your meaning! . . . And let it close, upon this dream in which you are enclosed, with the centuries and the dead, let close the Poem of Death where the Shadow shall have reigned.

THE HEROES

Of the obscure work of three centuries, what the world did not wish to be said is now said: heavy fighting was the only mark of time. Therefore, to evoke that obscure epic—Delgrès: struggled unto death against forces far superior in number and weapons. Perhaps his example infused the will of— Toussaint: who died for the same cause, and whose most famous lieutenant was of course—Dessalines: whose legacy was terrible . . . But upon these ravaged Indies, what miracle, or rather what necessity laid its toilsome hand? What was desire, madness and thirst for knowledge, fervor for gold and pleasure in triumph, took shape . . . Before, it was the unalterable mother, infusing speech—a Woman who was seen rising up in the dawn. What did she become? At last, the Poem shall tell.

LIII

She appeared in the morning; blind day nonetheless bedazzled, and
  futile; splendor having taken the east.
O birth! Upon a path in April; upon the locks of May when solitude
  is fragile; but also in the chaste sea burned by her lips.
She raises the cup of sand, her breasts gleaming, and while drunk she
  imbibes the azure and its miserable foam. May she come forth.
Saying: "You shall know me at the bottom of day. The sun is my
  companion," may she come.
The world applauds. Death comes in and plays. The azure turns pale.
  I tell you, abashed beauty was reassured and bedazzled.
(Her breasts flow from blind day, when she excites all that pain and
  all that noise.)

LIV

Such splendor was necessary, and such language, language that does
  not err; and splendor has its enticements. The Indies are imaginary,
  but their revelation is not.
She comes, and I follow her, I become drunk, until night when she
  enters the forest, leaving me at its border.
I know then that I endure no suffering which is not a border; which is
  not a cup of sand before the gulp of seas.

And shall I follow her? heart full of obscure reams (when the day is
    deserted and distraught in my noon, I weep),
She, the one I shall know at the end of this song, but so dazzling in
    her tears already,
That the day, when she appears, actually goes blind.
And there is more than one people who would drink of the azure
    within her!

LV

The man presses her against him, seeing in her only the mystery of
    her lips, jaspers of foam.
The sleep of night is late exhausted in her breast; he makes from it
    the aroma with which he perfumes the old remainder of his dream:
    this before, with one laugh, she gives light to the day.
He caresses her, there on her belly, near the wave, and he knows not.
    O tumults! O waves! O tides!
Perhaps she goes down into the night where dreams wander.
Perhaps she is suddenly there on the ridge, weeping.
His dream is of sweat and wisdom of the real; of wisdom.
And of obscure crimes on the outskirts of life.

LVI

On the clay bank, where the red wind insinuates itself, first there were
    a thousand rigid brilliant frostings smoldering incubations and
    mute beneath their ash of death.
The water of prophets has dried up in the urn; there are only
    imperfect lyres, and all the bells are silent.
Beneath the ash of death, along the ages that wove the foliated night,
    in the ardor of this night is still a people who are earnest.
And at noon, when the man marries his beloved,
Above the marriage vows could be heard the voices of those who came
    on the ocean; They do not seek their Indies. It is here.
"Ah," cried the woman, "the man is greedy before the crowd of his
    dream . . ."
She does not know that the man is, at crossings, a place of torches of
    the past that give off smoke with the wind.

LVII

Yet she embellishes the rumor of battle on the bank where she shines.
  And one may surprise at her side
The dreamy dying Indian who contemplates her, O silence,
The people of the evening, come from the forest, glimmerings,
And the sons of the Orient whose obolus is wisdom.
There will be sweat, much blood, and some cries.
So shall death fall into night.
We will know that the woman who awakens is Liberty, gentle or
  torrid, at the end of day.
(But it is already time to avow her.)

LVIII

Woman! from now on, before day, before the dark leaves, they come,
Your sons, and your guardians too, for whom a destitute Indies shall
  have grown
Into Gehenna and torrid forest, without border, in which each people
  kneels
When commence the somber ceremonies of its combat, and let the
  clouds rise!
From the depth of their assembly, those who thought themselves
  armed, the Voice of the flamboyant trees
And those who know you in the slip of their nights, do not know
  you!
They rise up here, and their name dazzles the Poem.

LIX

Toussaint, already named, who was a centaur, came to die on the
  frozen sand of the Empire.
In truth, your most difficult son; for him you veiled your face and
  spent your tears.
He knew you, then went away, at peace; you shall mourn upon the
  forest of cuscus the blood of your eldest son.
For he was on the ocean, against the grain of beginning
On his way to know the country of conquerers, from whence would
  rise the black fray of their crimes

(Now we can say that he was both sage and victim),
And history closed, upon this betrayed warrior, the unmindful curtain
  of a winter.
Let him die, oh let him die, and let the forest grow.

NOTE

Toussaint was called a centaur because he was inseparable from his horse.
cuscus: A type of tree.

LX

Shadow of blood, sprung from a lake of blood, pitiless: Dessalines.
This one was terrible. How many tears did he cost you, O priestess.
(Still, tell us! dogs fed on black men, if the sky was not tearful when
  they blessed you like a pack from Sologne! Before you went after
  the prey, did they not lock you up for three days without water?—
  and for meat, you had only what you caught.)
Dessalines, dog against dogs, was kept far from meat a whole
  lifetime.
He never drank any but the fetid water of combat, when even sweat
  turns gangrenous. Woman,
You wept over his hatred, and grow strong on his love.

NOTE

Sologne: A region of France known for boar hunting with packs of dogs.

LXI

Oh in the ages of these centuries, more eternal than the speech of the
  Oracles,
So did I see them, legion among the sprouts and brambles.
History forgets them, for they died on the side of the world where the
  sun sets.
I call out to them on the sands, near those who came to the New
  World, but in their hearts remained in the Old.
They are Conquerers of the denuded night. Open the doors and ring
  the bells for the somber heroes. The sea

Welcomes them among its sons, the sun rises on the breath of their
    soul.
They call to each other, the famous, and the forgotten, those who
    resisted the boatman of the caravels.
Their procession enters the scene, they have brandished torches of
    bamboo, and here is the first one,
Delgrès, who held Guadeloupe for three years.

NOTE

caravels: Ships used to transport slaves.

LXII

The wind comes down from the volcanoes, O wind, mare of lands!
    and the mind has no longer any breath which is not
Breath of lavas, of torments, breath of unpunished mouths and
    harvests of fires!
But the man knows then which way is North and where is the Death
    of his story . . .
There is an Indies which finishes when reality brushes its arduous
    hair; a land of dream.
It accepts what comes, suffering or joy, which is multiplicitous on
    the clay,
(Halfway between each of the races, mixing them).
From the dream described there, a high ground has come forth,
    which must be described,
Its richness is to name every ferment and every ear of corn and
    wheat.
Land born from itself, rain of the Indies they adopted.

LXIII

Woman, there are still those who placed the trace of their mouths
    upon your face.
They assemble in the clearing, swearing fidelity to the day and the
    clouds,
What do they need from this voice I have made my own, from the
    snow of this poem,

Except that every pith has consented to their service, and that in the
    forests where I penetrate now
The nearby foliage trembles on the verge of this memory?
From this edge of wood, they have made a beach, between the thorn
    and the bulls.
Their tide is made of the sapwood of the future, in which what Indies
    rustles?

NOTE

the thorn and the bulls: According to Glissant, this refers to a pasture which
contains bulls, surrounded by thorny shrubs.

LXIV

And look, there through the woods, the others who tremble softly,
Fearing to venture out or to approach the gods of fire and night.
Oh in the ages of these centuries, these others who bore fodder upon
    the litter of their masters, accepting
In words rich with spit, words of mud, the old vow of servitude,
They are like sarcasm, a wrinkle on the pond when others were
    bathing there!
For them at last the clearing opened, and we found that it was the
    temple
Of your sons, O Liberty, of your guardians from that time, while as a
    woman you recline beneath the branch,
And the bird of paradise refolds his billows of fervency.

RELATION

The poem is finished when the shore, from which the Discoverers formerly departed, comes into sight. Return to this strand, where the cable is still fastened. What wealth has burgeoned in the course of the cycle? Who returns? And that man there, what does he, in his turn, covet? But perhaps after all man has only the same desire and the same fervor, whoever he is. And no matter where he comes from, the same recognizable suffering? What Indies call to him? Or, if his dream is already no more than an impassioned reason, what ocean yet stands between him and it—? No one can say with certainty; but everyone attempts the new crossing! The sea is eternal.

LXV

From the prow of the ship to the blade of chalk is a moat, the last one.

The sea, more mountainous, and more miserly with silence, is
   obscurely
Agitated against the plain where glory dies, between the field and the
   crows.
There! Let the call finish upon this world, in its shadowless
   geography! Oh may it be exhausted! And let there be neither atoll
   nor bay in desire
(Yesterday the last island was peopled with cartographers and engineers,
They have measured every dimension of the statues of Easter Island)
To inflame sailors and monks, pilgrims of the Garden of Gold.

A watery barricade (just one, O my weariness?) after these nights and
   dawns in splendor and waiting on the sea.
Once more I salute the dawn that is burgeoning upon an unknown
   poem and upon desire;
Soon the plain will have circled in one swoop of wings what was
Mountain and sea of hope, and harbor of desire where suffering lies.

But where, oh where do the sails die, worn out with wind?
The chimneys, open to the voiceless azure,
No longer cry out their blue smoke. For one more time

There is yet one ship's boy on the bridge who is not steering the
    cables toward the dock (he is too young, ungainly)
But he smiles at the knot of gray water on the hull, unlacing its
    thickness . . .
Three centuries have bound this coming in straw and sand,
Not fallen from the mast, but stranded in an unspliced, reefless clarity
(An island only just appeared, born upward by a seism like a flower
    on the water
Before falling back toward the deep corals)
Stranded, peasant of the ancient Indies, son of the land of the past
    which once was the land of the future.
Soon the plain, the fields of gold, through which a city appears!

Genoa! you hearken in the night of the horizon, O ritual city!
Is it finally you on the plain, to offer the entire unique adventure
In each stone of your streets, the fragile flight of the epic
More delible in the face of your piers than in the memory of
    your sons?

So! let us shout the Precursors and those who sailed other seas in
    the airlocks of their madness
Their names were omitted, but are they not entitled to appear at the
    end, while the city hibernates,
Those who first left the mark of their gloves upon the map?
Polo, the illuminator, who spoke of the world and filled it with
    wonders.
Gama, dazzling panicle and squat glory, risen from a pedestal of
    water.
Magellan, whose name scourged the very storm and deracinated
    Six-masts—
What did they ever nourish but the land as prophet, dream's
    alluvium?

(What did they violate, who passed so closely by the immured,
    immuring them?
And their face bore not the silvering of a single gaze, they who
    gazed.)

City. I gaze at you above the thick aggregation of madness and life, in
these three times one hundred years.
Again you are a city for the widow's gaze, after the nuptial of
adventure!
There are only fields of undulating wheat where were the prairies of
the hurricane, alas
There are but tears of the factory and batteries of pain where the
heroes arose.
Here, the creed of these people is in naming every leaven and every
panicle
And your people, not decked out for the departure of solemn seamen,
At noon when the sea blesses the crowd—
But feeling that gentleness and aware of that pain in the batteries of
streets.

A watery barricade (the last, O my fatigue?) and the procession
toward the dock is slow.

From everywhere, oh from everywhere, this lament of the world that
inebriates
The lungs—and yet which traces out hope.
The undulating wheat, the moat, and the dock of dead wood,
The plain where the cities are, all Genoas on their wharves,
And an Indies, which? in which the dream has its alluvium.

It is thickness of sky and the last coveted star,
It is, in a corner of the moon, the oasis of the infinite
It is liberty nourishing humankind, it is the woman beloved
It is for a grieving people the opening of the undergrowth,
For someone dying it is silence and for the living, beauty
And in the heart, it is the knot of gray water that lies in wait.

There! no more plain! Where is the city? ah, convoy your armadas
upon the new empire,
Frigates! A new Indies, of disproportionate reason, has taken the sea
With its prescient men. They remember those who waxed eloquent
About glory and fragility on the first beach.

Here is the beach, the new one. And it advances heavily into the tide,
The sea! oh here it is, wife, at the prow, giving up the anchor.
She rolls, quite level: on her unplundered way.

O journey! These forests, these virgin suns, these waves
Are one and the same efflorescence! Our Indies are
Beyond all rage and acclamation, these are left behind on the shore,
Dawn, radiance sailing the wave henceforth
Its Sun, of splendor, inured mystery, O ship,
Rugged calm of the horizon amid an uproar of currents,
And the eternal fixity of days and tears.

BLACK SALT

to the sea

For the salt it signifies.
Splendor and bitterness yet again. Affliction of lights upon the expanse.
Profusion. Theme, pure idea, bound with sea foam, with salts. Monotony:
tireless clamor ruptured by the cry.
There is—on the delta—a river where the word accumulates, the poem—
and where salt is purified.

The First Day

   The storyteller measures his voice by the disproportion of its brilliance. He will, in utter solitude, sing the earth, those who suffer through it. He does not offer his voice to those it pleases, those who are exalted by it; but to bodies burned by time: thickets, confined people, naked villages, the shore's multitude.

   When this wise sailor, careful speaker, is completed by his song, it recommences him. He arrives, a child, in the first morning. He sees the initial sea foam, the salt's first sweat. History, waiting.

I

   The mud slides down the mornes reddening the blades of cane.
Presence, O waves! A man governs the mists of torches with his speech, he sees
   The image that his heart and his words have conjured.
He ties the night among canes and waters. He speaks clay on the body and then this word.
   He cries out.

Amid such weeping, I listened to the night.

II

Ancient times. Nubile times. Riddled with distances. Masts!
The first salt in the hollow of a weary hand.
O light, morning that raises you upon your years.

A huntsman cries with astonishment, he departs
With the taste of dreams and bitterness on his skin,
Dawn vacillates, ah the beauty of withdrawing
Through the sea of silence and the brilliance of your fluency,

Dawns! As for me,
I regret nothing. Time is there.
Other stars will sing
In the voracious darkness of this towpath.

III

Men will go down this road of mud, they will enlist, willingly they will expose their bodies to lengthy work. The midday wind covers the roofs, women raise into their eyes a pure brilliance, dogs head to the sea (where await radiant feasts of dung and parasites).

Look, the sea has carried me off toward fertile day, oh from so far away again I move with the tides toward this absence and this face.

And if all you retain from my words is this taste of tangled lands, I have not wasted my time nor spun in vain the straw of my heart.

IV

The priest recites his knowledge to the luminous trees.

And they tell him: this language that seizes you is not from you, dig for your words.—He says:
I have no utterance beyond this shoreless river, where mires rise. They swell, while mud envelops us. Who speaks to us of digging?
In the thick waves I heard these words. I was the sprout that grew, far from any gold, I was pollen and wind. The sea gathered clay and the entire island capsized.

The priest recites his wisdom, and thusly the earth turns, and from below leaves are seen in their somber verdure.

V

Unbind your soul, stand, and contemplate this land.
Cloistered death
Divides us, and your eyes have sealed
mourning.
Only through your gaze may we enter, yet it remains
closed. For us,
Only your face will take its part in the wedding. Your face
alone.

Who are you? The horizon can barely hold you. The
plain
    You see released into this dawn so pure
    Cries death to us, with all its entablatures of mire.
    Who are we, in this clay where blood
flows?

    The song purifies you, you falter. Only your memory
grows.

VI

    Unbind your soul, earth, moored to your cry.
    Imminent, eternal, observe. I see winter grow here
    And your heart at its highest midpoint. The old
brilliance

    Ripens. The old love subsides.
    Open up to us the relief of your dying roads.
    You were salt in the snow and the snow was but night.

VII

    Kingdom that cries out in marble, in hearths.
    Silos that tempted me through long nights.—I
have seen night.

    Be bright and bare, so that with one hand the man sweating in the
field of cane may offer you a place of fury, of friendship.
    He has already cut six times twenty bales for the baling woman.—
And I say: Give
    That I may be as murky as this pretemporal night
    Whatever is muddy suits us, lunatic managers,
unscramblers of
    Worlds, chaos, swords knotted in the naked sky. And I answer:
    Winter who grasps me from under your cloud, I have seen
    How rare this passion and how profound this tide.

VIII

Obscure schemes rose up out of the branches
They were birds, wings, noises hardly beginning,
A commotion, but the bank merely rustled, open skies
Gave way to passion. It was dawn.
And the sword. The wake. A bright town hauling
Its roofs and heaps of straw into the sky.

My only cry is in this trace the salt has left.

IX

Each dawn this word delves deeper and deeper into the thickets,
climbing vines, and sand. Into the sea.

Gentle, lovely people, so tenacious and calm,
I hear people, the splendor, I hear them.

You must name them. Shout them. Time is there. Summer has spread
Across the snow like a black absence.
At last, with these words, the day is illuminated.

X

Depths O tides.
Birds, dying at our sides, with this rumor of the past
Towns, weary rivers, so many fruits, so many swords.

You become a mirror for this face, the sea's magnificence, like a harsh
gale between life and us
And the grieving wind in its madness O wind.

You become a face where this mirror fades and you
More ardent than our voices in this passage of time
Become a voice for the hunter who hears you.

XI

And here you are now, salt from the realm of my hands. I am as one,
Dumbfounded, plunging into the sea, who watches perish
Night and shorelines around him, the words
Of torches, like a flower, mute like the current.

And who is reborn on the morning of the first day. He knows
The sparkling night, the braziers, the only fruit.

XII

Like one born on a boat amid the brilliant trees.
It is the final night. Tomorrow stone by
stone
    Will be selected. Like one sculpting a bone out of blue sulphur,
    He sings the bitter night open to the salt and a
woman
    Sadder than the sun's nubile body burning,
    When its fire, dying within itself,
is altered
    Amid the day and its illumination.

Carthage

Salt already on the hands of the gravediggers. The sea's scum, no longer a fragrance, is spread over the conquered city. One forgets the first salt he tastes: behold him trafficking its essence. The world—and today one sees countless more plundered Carthages—feeds this fire within him to conquer, to kill. The docile sea is his accomplice.

A people arrives; and is rationed its share of salt upon the labor of its wounds. At last free it laments upon ashes. Salt is forever mixed with the victims' blood and with injured stones that were the toil of men.

I

Soldiers have built cities around the globe, corrupt with girls who lay down in this filth, both girl and city. Ships' bows till the sea, shouting the fear of it to their prows: dogs are coming! And men follow from behind, legions.

Stand. Beware. City, you are already burning. Behold.
Dogs, men, beauties, your heart perishes so soon.

II

In this heart were glory, edges, black sand
In this heart were silence: agonies deliriums deaf beasts.
There morning sweats yesterday's blood into rock.
Within this heart is a heart of enormous granite, a word. The woman
Letting slip the veil of her dress in his hands
Suddenly leaves the flash of this road, surrenders
So as not to hear the city's pleading at the foot of the rocks.

III

She travels by sea, and praying to roots,
Flees far from this word and falls to the sand.
She falls. Unknown beauty from the sea, wreck
and gift of a truly sordid wedding in our midst Ah
You are purified by water, ravished by its foam. Abruptly,
Night falls upon you. Here is the spear, the tracked woman, the blood.
A woman at your feet crying for mercy, conquerors.

IV

Can you articulate this city, its looming storm
And walk along the rocks off Numidia
And the door closed slowly and the old
men
    Nailed to the wall by drunken soldiers and the man
    Who sits on the tower, indifferent, repulsed by his own
soul
    The lingering cry of children hurled into this sea?

I have seen the cold sea that churns, waits, subsides
And takes an ancient salve into its flesh,
young flesh
    As an offering, something due, or a sacrifice in the strong
south wind
    Calmer in its immense reception and more
temperate
    Than the November sky where vultures mate.

V

The sea cries but the sea soon fades. And the
soldier
    Inflates it with corpses, violent itching. It willingly
    Receives the payment for its toll, and is hired out
    Indebted with life whose stunned display ebbs away
    Along the shore, where this joyous hymn lies dying. A word
    Awaits you, you have not yet emptied the cup, you are bound by a
word
    You, sea. And a hundred furies will turn blue from this
butchery
    Before your solemn foam begets gold
    So that the City in High Season may dazzle.

VI

Between me and my life lies this specter of my life
Murdered forsaken an unwieldy love rising beneath the waters,
Night has taken this city by force
I stand watch silently from the besieged tower

I see legions oh solitude buzzards
And the slave lying with his throat slit while the master wears his
blood: a costume
Bereft of irony: dogs! And blood worthy of
blood.
Bitter smoke shrouds the red morning, the impenetrable night.

Defiled corpses, iron muzzles, the fire's froth
Entrails strewn along the fire's edge, a
woman
Running from the sea, hoping to reach the flames, behold
her
Exposed, arms reaching for the horizon. Between my
life

And me a black expanse opens up, I reach out my hands,
I cry
Into the fire which is eternally rekindled.

VII

Towers collapse, gold falls away, even the
lords
But there were slaves a whole lot of them who
ran away
In the complicit night to the south and the forest, Oh night.
And the conquerors loudly erase any sign of
humanity
Piling jewels, washing blood from the pearls
They coldly calculate, argue, dogs
bark
(Throw them a scrap, they'll eat it without even knowing what it is!)

Sea wind solemn sea wind covers the city its invisible
blue fingers
    Caress the decomposed, the insanity of it all, the sullied wind
    Like a woman reaching toward the horizon.

VIII

    Grasses no longer weep beneath the wind. Nothing stirs not
seaweed
    Nor Sacred Altars that stand amid ashes
nor
    The Port where the peddlers stand watch. (And the
Altar
    Pronounced: I am the flame of the hearth—
The Port
    Opened each morning to goods
from the Orient.)

    Listen, city, beneath the silence, to a wave a cry
    That almost vanish only to reemerge, you shudder
    The sap opens a bay a breeze a lily within you
    Noon carves out dry and infinite things upon the heights.

IX

    Salt! O salt and whiteness, heart of famine, impure
toil
    Naked shadow from which the woman fled so long ago! Word
from the sea,

    Uproar! And the bramble without soil, hard death,
cloth
    Bleached by noon, O wound. And the Roman,
man of boredom: proclaims
    Here will be a lake and a mirror, parched gulls
    Will come and circle forever.—
You, sea
    This is the last gasp of your revelry. You have come into this eternity to
cherish
    The solemn silence you once were.

X

You shout your solitude into this glacier that is you. And the
man
   Made immensity his slave, and the sea his fruit.
   He called out, and your strength obeyed, in the hand of a hostage
   Who scattered it on the walls, on the earth and
on
   The blanched eyes of a corpse that we slowly turn over.

   Have you come to die in this wreckage or to see for yourself
   The lushness of a place built upon salt? Have you come to
see
   The extent of this blood poured down your paths:
whiteness
   Where at times nothing grows but bursts of inebriated light. And I
   Will remove from your eyes the taste of darkness made safe, so in
     the end
   You mourn this blood, this place, this corpse.

XI

   One cries for salt as if for a vanished woman, pale
Scipio
   Laments your soul while he mocks it. Will you let
   This sad creature contemplate the deserts you've begotten, saying:
   How peaceful is my repose upon a bed of terrors—
   Then he tastes the salt, thinking of the Games he will
give.

   Will you always let the enormous rapture of your
cry
   Die at the feet of a man drunk on the blood of others?
And you
   Will you always give your body, this blaze of
viscera,
   And the road of your barrenness, to someone
   Who grows tired with this diversion in his glory and desire?
   The sea grown silent, flees. And traces of its foam stay with me.

XII

Men, lancers, run away. And the
dogs. O city
    Silence and death now render you so pure. The slave
    Leaning toward the cry from your shroud, says
    The sea finally calls! And its foam in one's hand is
    Like a rock where wind has placed many dawns, a
black salt.

    The sea labors beneath the prow. A cry arisen. The
woman
    Dragged against the wind swears and bites and laughs at last.

Salt Taxes

Thatched hut. Straw and mud. The king's cavalry in the distance. The father wants to protect his crumbling shack, but how? They will burn his feet, hang him from a tree until he speaks. The wife hides her treasures: cauldrons, bowls, hoes. A young boy roots among the firewood, soon he will bury it in a sack in the meadow. The Dragoons will pillage and burn. The donkey will perish, the mother weep, the oldest son be taken away.

So, cry for this soil. Imagine it near a sea it has never known. Let another come from farther away and teach. When permitted, time makes knowledge and salt seasons it.

I

I have seen you glean your bodies, you were skeletons, Dead men with fruitless scythes yielding only the harvest of your bones. When you hid the dreary treasure of your chaff, praying the smell would reach the heavens, beyond human nostrils, I was at the edge of your toil. I saw your bodies, dark fruits, and the Dragoons feeding on them. I have known you as the incense of their amusement; you were streets for their marching! Oh until your own death sweltering death pursues you. Gruel is your lot. A hounded voice your lay. People of the country of France, those whom you levied in the damp of autumn: to die there among falcons and bramble.

II

Peasants, I awaited you by the seas. Behold this eager
face.
Followed by rocks. The unhinged foam.
Like traces on the sea of an immense flight of October birds.
Night dies in the day, want dies in its ford.

Thus the tragic death thus the smells of drought
Die, to make acquaintance at sea.
And you, the living in the radiant death.

—Who, the one calling out? What sea hovers above?
And summons us to cleanse the tower in a fire of oaks?

I am the somber witness, the mandate. You are
Bitter hands singing in a bitter eddy.
And you,

In this lightning and confusion you are
Speechlessness emptiness the storm
Where the black silence that grips me cries out.

III

Night scarcely molted, half closed, surprises
The topsoil: the part of me that slaves, frets,
and cries.

Time shifts its soft wings, the sheet of dreams
Drape it over the sea, to lull and conceal.

Time cries: You are but furies on their way to the
shore.
Voracious questions, famines, and tracks of frenzied birds.

IV

And reply. The sea eludes us, gone is the horde of
ship stays,
Toward a beloved sun, a July, children.

Its beaches cry music for those whose souls are
ephemeral,
Who, taking the sea in their hands, concede. The sea runs away.
But the song's foam is fragile, man yields to it.

You are hands slashed in lunacy
Clever peasants trampled by horses, and
crazed lovers eager to break their chains
Women bared at the king's command
Embezzlers of salt with neither salt nor fodder. I see
Other muzzles, hands dead without a sound.
I cry. May beauty befall you!
You who recognize salt in its sudden darkness.

V

As salt escapes from the bastion of day
And dries in the hand where the sea
Placed the foam of its breast
And just as no one will drain the night, nor anyone
Drink of love from this hand,

Thus I have vainly taken wood away from your cinders
Watched over your barns, your harvests, and your locked food stores.
And dawn remained vacant and the rose ever more dessicated.

VI

The only sound is that of blood convoyed by the sea. The only storm
is one of blood.
The bitter odor draws near, breathe it in, my surging tides. There is
no sound
But that of the faint incense of people caught in the fire of our time
Who die while bringing the depth of seas and the stench
Of the most distant planets.

VII

Thus near rocks once hurled into the sky, that fell
Like melancholy games of a titan or foams left by this
love
I see the air throbbing with burns, I see the stubbled
field
The fresh earth where salt was left, the stable of
waves
For a horse hacked to pieces, neighing amid the
flames
For a heart ripped to shreds slowly sinking beneath the
sand
Like the savage toys of a hurricane, swallowed up.

VIII

May beauty befall you, peasants. You within this book—
beneath the kings, priests, captains, blood and quicksilver of fame—
where you wander, saying
    Who will turn our wounds into wisdom? Who will turn our famines
into fines? And dredge up our silvering?
    (Still saying: Oh! May the wind never cease.)

    And I shall tell of you Serfs and Martyrs, fires,
vow
    So very black. And other gods and the highest rank.

IX

Grooms mocked before the wedding, where only the wife attended the
feast, History
    That let down its hair, gave birth to swine,

    I cry out this word, desert in which you stray, jungle
    Striped by your nephews' sword, doing what they did to you. Where
is the salt

    That made you suffer greatly and with such fervor?

X

They leave, at times calling out, and at times gathering this dust from
the sea. There aren't any food stores now, no salt, no barn; and dried is
the rose. I stand, hailing the remainder of the day. Peasants, at your side
stands one not of your blood, burning the tide as he goes. He sees the
woman above the city, with girders for her fiery mane. She is a victim
of Legions, rose of the sea. And huntress near the tide, seeking neither
salt nor firewood. She held out her hand, in which the sea suddenly
sparkled, the sea we have so much inveighed. There we spy from the
distance this forbidden Salt, being carried off to the shores of morning.

Africa

    I saw the distant land, my light. Belonging only to those who fecundate her: within me, and not I in her.

    The tribes waged war for control over salt; nations rise to learn its flavor. May the laborers of night also drink from this fountain of morning. Another land beckons.

    It is Africa, yet it is not. For me it was a silent land. Listen. Everybody dances, in the righteousness of his own body and voice, in honor of the eternal fire.

Oho O woman who has come undone, see how you splatter
At last I know the weary child who grieves within you
I recognized the man who will supply you with
    ocean
Beside him sea-draped walks the African woman
The one who dares to name her, she answers, and he sees his queen

Oho Handmaid for so long you were turned into exile
And magnificent desire yet desire absence and oath
As though from a dream, where there was a queen but no
    royalty
But now the sleeping man weeps, at his feet the evening sun
Weaves death together with the naked tree, bearing neither fruit nor
    resting-place

And you stood watch O distant one though not beautiful
Your beauty penetrated beneath the skin worse than a
    cry
You made mayhem out of so much brooding your beauty
Flowed formlessly in swells and chastely hunted clouds
You the shadow the fury you the slow waning of water

Crying out the scent, praising the deed, measuring the wrath,
Or disrupting the bursting light of your peaks this is not my purpose
Nor is stirring the perfumes that form your somber
    entourage

I haven't your forests' verdict branded on my body
Nor have I your salt in my eyes unless it is an imagined salt

Oho unnamed Mother of deeds named by
My heart, you the secret heart of this voice, listen I
  cry out
Without seeing if the sun is evening yet, without resolving
If the word is now cleansed of its torture, see
I have now left the flame the rites the brilliance

And they told me: Listen well, this song is not a poem,
But a parable, an object of its surroundings. Have they
  counted
The stanzas that death sings before us?
  Have these
Lords with no lands, seen this face's fire, its throbbing?
They told me it was a lie, and the sad universe lies to them

Gathering this river as I travel to where you settled like silt before me
To me you've been a river since I began collecting
  rivers
Like a bouquet of pounding flames, like a
  mass
Of divided tears not yet exhausted by impatience
And I saw the immense surge of your cry tremble

In the distance I saw the dawn that you'd become.
In pale green droves, night watched over the world,
  then wind
Entangled our eyes. For your sake, mother, we believed.
  Must we
Once night and wind fuse their nakedness together
Sculpt flowers, polish clouds, bemoan the dogs howling?

And all this noise from the waking world, fallow
After a long massacre and an even longer sleep, the
Fierce fire enamored with your dawns, the sky hurled

From crime to crime toward your imagined summits, child
Sky, vast body that the star will soon unbridle

Oho mother O regent in your secret burning
Dreamed of for so long and concealed for so long
You now open the tree where desires sleep
The queen rises within you, here, in your cry I set out
And like seaweed, moor my cry to your root

You are murky weather and blurring light oho
You make me thirst for you whom I have not tasted thus you were
Distant and obscured by words this sentinel
Within me, gesturing, cried out poverty to days without
    praise
Beckoned the topsoil and the dogs drunk from sleeping upon it

I hear the year pounding its feeble cry upon your paths
I hear the slow drum of uprooted lands I hear
The land inside the mouth and the honest word
The ceremonial drumming of tribes declaring
    war again, and it is
Heat from the salt on the enemies' pagan hands
    Feel

Grueling need racks your body in vain, famine
Where winds javelins seas and furors grow, startled forests
The wind's loose knots lick the hearth, children
    cry out
A hut burns, a warrior dies, pastures
    smoke
Famine in the scorched sky, and famine in your vigor

And in the wax-sealed, monotonous word I hear famine
Oho words of our blood that now pound against
    time
Of days dangled fourteen times in horrific fire

I see this heart braided with fire, charred days,
   blood
And to these spoils a bit of salt tasting of burned grass

Those who came to salt like dogs to quarry
You had no sky night kindler or spear
Even the night left you, even night, you burned
Forests suns and winds on the ends of your javelin
They made cargo of your children's naked flesh

The skies held you in their green boughs for so long
Salter of this body of whose years drank up bewildered women
Fountain that you scattered amid the devastation you cried
Uprooted life, you cried, starless sky
And we, impure cadastres out at sea, in knots of islands

For this unsilvered salt rationed out by paladins
Knights of blood beneath their wine-rusted shields,
For this plunder which you gleaned on the field of history
When they harvested their glory without glory oho
So many incinerations of lepers so much night, without absolution

Oh you are Voice, and their arrogance will dry up. They stand
Before the naked brilliance and amid red bays, wind
From seas hurled against corals and gulfs
Where more than one people has plowed beauty and crests
Lost lost voiceless victims nights desires
   trembling

Oho you carder of wool it is time to untangle this time, to weigh
With sea to measure with black salt
Sown with the blood of peoples who have all perished,
Your only mother is beauty dredged up on you from
Torrid seas and blue frosts of springtime
   Hear

A Ship! Which tethers nights and summons us imperiously
Time within all flesh, new shoots latent in every clutter of seeds
Lands have crumbled from this voice, it is poetry
And a road raised between us and the sea, to you
Pledged to time and voice that beseech for all

You leave guns spears and seas at the door
At the place where salt was pillaged from you, you begin to sing
The place patient with sea and survival
For all a world and a vine where at last time unfurls
The space is solemn within us, woman, the sea is strong

Africa Africa O most joyous stanza O impenetrable beauty
I dreamed, humanity fastened its heavy exile within you
Now I have renounced coarseness and dullness for the smooth face
Gypsum for iron and coral for fish
Here, the weir is bare, behold the African woman upon the sand

And she takes salt into her hair beautiful jay beautiful fruit
And perhaps we will finally collect it all, oh perhaps.

Wounds

We move along this tilling; we know we have the same duration or the same heaviness. We cry out for salt. It is useful on wounds. It is good for torturing.

(I saw the sages who did not succumb to beauty. They believe they weigh their words, hoarding their potbellied boredom.)

Beauty, distant from our sea: we must confess why your face is soft, yet your hands hard, and now your body gnarled, on the embers of our fires.

Beauty, beauty again for unknown stars, beauty for peoples. And salt within the seed, and rain for unscathed lands.

I

Once again on our lips there is a cry for oats, for death.
The year grazed upon its ashes the shore
Left its sand to the ruins of the sea.

Oh the slow expanse is given to us with
only foam.
The foam escapes. And we grow silent
We see this procession where beauty's flame
Was deserted.

We see the city pass by with its charred prows. Shout
So that the procession will notice us. Hail them. Silence, solemn
passage.

(Flame, beauty O woman, they have forgotten us).

II

This wind hauled up into your hair
Immediately bonds wind with this fire
You play land and water on your sand
A nocturne that has found its way through a quaint doorway
You are my night my land my vow.

If I speak of you as dead inanimate
You form an impromptu sun within your fires
To torment the body in which I rest.
Even dead you are not lost,
Your body I love is the body of day.

III

They have passed, princes of the sea
They have released us from the secret bay.
We count the sands with the foam
The terror, the secret hope. Splendors
Of sparkling mirrors. Birds so very dark.

Horde! Sunset where the heights slope downward! Bloody sailing ship.
Thus history passed. Far from this sand where we stand watch.
An island
   Beckons us. We answer. Blood, naked lavas on the
setting sun. Space
   Where the house passes, birds—the stutterer
calls out to you
   But he will not enter the wayward season.

Even had he seen, when nights were illuminated,
even had he seen,
   What could he have seen? Seeing the woman who to him is
not woman but beauty
   Had he seen the woman, even so, what would he say, seeing such
beauty pass by
   The woman, who is one, attended, sky and fire
passing? If he had seen
   The woman pass like a wax seal on a peaceful year, far from the sand?

And if he had even seen beauty itself passing by?

IV

I am of night but all made up you
Remain far from my nocturnal cries,
The tides open me so that I may see you
At nighttime yesterday they turned me into a crowd
Deprived of merriment and gifts for an entire year.

A single bloody January lingers eternally
To tarnish you
It is an edge bereft of gold and a white quarry
O beauty that howls as it climbs the swelling waves.

V

He saw the procession of princes and courtiers pass. Swords bloomed.
He saw the evening's blade blaze in the evening's blood. Also
Victims towing the sturdy vessel and at the prow fat bankers
Making stars unstruck with flesh and fruit.

He saw their counting scales on the uppermost deck. Magi passed
Declaring the ocean waters eternal
They filled the sea with a wake of words. Adrift on
shore
He saw time, splendors, nudities.

This breath of beauty on her face.
The faceless woman who filled red sails with her breath. Then
he had
A vision of the wound on his heart, not the wound itself but its seal

Thus he saw within himself the woman stripped of adornment.

VI

I relegated you to impure hearths
Making you into the sound of my seas and you
Rare silence that passed within me
I captured silence in the snare of an alma

So gentle lover so weary of going to
What was the edge of this bitter mane
Here no shedding of tears seizes you, summer
Is clenched in these fires that were once your eyes.

VII

This impure cry. Clay where he placed his breath.
He said: Beauty
Of the world that capsizes all at once, pass on. The fire
Within you howls, it is an oath from the seas.

But his song is impure and his throat is knotted, inside him he sees
The woman then pass amid a long procession of setting suns.

Her hair sounds in the night they are tresses of
chains
Her hands bleed they are the hands of withered peoples
Her body bears the weight of time, mixed with blood
She has the dreaming eyes of the forgotten dead
Movements of girls dragged into the fire
Beauty beauty the world is there and it is your bruised body.

VIII

I named you beauty, entrusting you with this solemn
shriek of wings where you pass
With words heaped upon my fire by constant torment, I have named
you
Vertigo, you select me in the fluency of your speech, on the dying sea.

You took the wave in your fingers, interlacing foam with sky, making
Wreckage of these words that pound at your side. I named you
Beauty, woman, such a gentle swell, a path upon the setting sun, you
stirred up
Sea spray in the eye opened by this shore
Where I once knew the sea's past, azure
Where I saw you—cloaked in wounds.

There I came to know the fabric of wounds.

IX

Is there one, or who is it, who sings and is wounded
Far from us when the water yields
And am I in this sea and in the tide where the wandering woman
Grew weary? Or in a self who expanded an impure
space?

Or am I in this mirage of putrid curing salt
When only blood keeps us sane
And stagnant in the wound absence weeps where she
passes.

X

He said Asia, land of red water where embers
smolder.
    Dead islands, arms stretched out, their hands with burned palms,
    Hands that bind the sky with their fingerless palms
to a linen of ashes.

    The gaudy sun made a show of drinking the sea's humble blood, and
the man
    Thus dreamed of a hunt in which these stars served as prey, and
humankind as bait.

XI

Lands. Hushed roots, Africa and islands far from the name
Abandoned in the pangs of agony, banished from the world, naked
With blood obstructed by nights
He spies you Polynesia and dying and somber
And denies your hardship and sees you
without fruit
    As we see the rooster, in the gold of old corn,
    die a cruel and sparkling death.

High Noon

Then the sun, this solitary kingdom. That was once the land of childhood, which still is, quite simply. All this wounded time to arrive at the secret of salt kept by an island. This grand ambition to modify time. One can only stretch out the space within, where its word is reiterated, where its light rustles.

I saw my island on its sea wind. At last the poem's salt placed within the earth as it slows.

I

Gentle, lovely people, behold the azure.

Lovely, gentle toll, eternally falling from your cry. Where is your night's horseman? The stain on the mare's muzzle, as she assaults the rock? This one, more dismal than night, who swallows this blind wind whole, and who pleads—shouting out to you.

Where is this unseen dust that lay between the stones? And this tired child riding the mare. Only the hooves steady the stone.

And in your disheveled night there is no wind, sea, or mare with a stained snout,
Only when dawn takes the horseman by surprise.

II

The cliff has bound its nest of clay to the sea. At last the dock, long celebrated in the majestic city of his song. And sixteen times the wound on the fan of his hands. At last the sound of a moaning chain on the dock.

A cry not voiced, at the ships' arrival. Now the anchor is lowered into the immense gulp. The bay of prose not shouted with splendor or songs of oars or jetties, but with meandering and trunks and papers, to come ashore.

The sky tightens its throttle (the reef of the dock without thrust or brake) on the homeplace licked by water.

III

—The men came in, the blaze of sea is in their hearts.

And the best stood up, the glimmer of auguries in his eyes. Does he see, deep within his eyes, the proudest of forests? And he cries out: I proclaim you. O encircled, familiar woman

He did not run, a gust of foam on his mouth. Hear, he said, time cracking. It is the woman in his eyes.

Oh is she lying there, more naked than the smell of frying in the sea?

Body's drum and most beautiful bow, some men are approaching. But the best has not offered his voice.

IV

There was this bird, a solitary bird on our sand, and this woman in the song (no one will say whether it was a woman or a forest that fell in love), and there was this bitterness, a lone cloud, winnower of salt, like an oath from the sea that the shore does not hear—and there was the cold naked flower blooming from the stem, at the time when the sailing ships, leaving the wind, came back into the horizon of clays and oars.

There was this bird trembling, black intransience amid the trembling streams of West Africa.

V

This island, then these islands joined as one, Oh name them.

Proclaim them. All I want in the sea is a fold of clay that stands watch. An entire embankment of foam.

Where is the first? Where is the foreign woman with an ancient vow? An island, a wind?—And the sea lies. The vow fades. As the rooster is bound to his corn.

Endless slashers and slayers. Your clay has burned. Dead are your hands. Cry out the wind.

O sea, name these ghosts.

VI

Unbind your soul. So that a horseman pushing his beast at noontime may name you. And may he name you another celebration, far from the song.

And may he pause, the cavalier. He bends toward the moment, where foam embraced its salt. He ties his horse to a barren lemon tree. And sees the lucid flower on the cooking fire, the most green. He gazes at the demented wood.

Waves deeper than a fire. The sea calls, through a phosphorescent midnight.

He does not remember the moment, when the bird alighted.

VII

As the word flashes on the earth—and roots rise up to where the wind already blows.

(Let no bedazzled sleeper go there, or let him stay awake all day, who does not return with the bird of the past. Where are you, enormous birds?)

Birds of the wind that will soon die, where are you? Oh so many remains. Then the song, the ardent hoe.

On the one hand, objects of lightning, sea winds, the mocked sea. But on the other hand, the advancing poem.

(And even if there is a place the word does not know, it is apt this place, to commend it. For in the end this word knows its own sound. The nascent fire collapses on the bow of nights.)

Which, this splendor? Erecting its landscapes from one edge of the word to the other?

And these deserts appeared where the downpour lifted its veil.

Who is the one walking among earthly words, endlessly recommencing the step of the original syllable?

It is done, it succumbs, taking root in the air.

Among the roots, bound up with the immense wound, a man arose.

His place: triple-tiered bed of foams, the shores' muddy sword.

The Cove Lady where the water lay; and the Black Cove, its unraveled rope cramming the rock.

And the July sea preyed on by black bulls.

O for the slashers and singers we will have songs, as pure as Caesar-less black victories.

And for the slayers of noontime stains, a dewless song of roses.

—I rise and I explore and I embrace the unnamed country.

Acclamation

It was the salt in the basin of time. Nothing was left but an obscure urn of words. Is it morning? Darkness is certainly a good omen—when words shine on the flight of steps before the house. In this realm of our hands.

I

Bring me mires iron sheets mango trees from the blaze
Let the limpid word dry and the drought cease
Where straw was and every thing uncircled
It is time to stop the vast wandering and it is time
To arm the song with continents
That hail us as they pass in broad day
O worry, salt left by foam upon death, my black land.
Take me into the summer that has no spring, O cry.

II

It is the town, speechless in its clay. It is the green wood, where it props itself up onto night.

They are our dogs that we see lapping between two winds. Ragged dogs, emaciated sorcerers of our absence, stray dogs. It is women, fierce hungers, and men, toothless mouths. The factories' roux, the year's vintages. I have not named the sea that marries

A black cry, separated from the black procession. O this land
Closes the sea and against the sound of approaching peoples
Pulls shut its sandy grips, with their bolts of rock.

III

I made a home of such a cry, where no land rises; and no shoal approaches the seas where I have been.

Cast aside by the cyclone, he sees the mud at the door, the path leading to nights where each one wavers on the verge of death

And he hears the earth where more than one name was buried.

IV

Hear the lands, behind the islet.

YOKES

for every country that turns away
and grows exasperated to discover that it is running dry

YESTERYEAR

Gorée

He lived his cry which was an entire tree: his roots shouting flowed into ravines.

He wove the crudeness of depths into the canyon of time, and with his gaze stayed many a windless sail.

He had no room to cry out that they had gone too far, having steered between coast and bluffs, into the sheltering island where dreams of the past strangle the dreams of tomorrow to death.

Burned Field

yoke
shackle
fetters
iron collar (pepper gag, nailed ear)
the four posts
the twitching

we do not trace the scars of our stripes

Fats

In a gust of gasping greenery, behold at eye level the salty boredom of white butter flow, plump princess, and this worker stiffening as she praises the marks of thrown pucks, a penny's worth of lard, and next to it the humble wad of fat beaten red: our empty mouths.

We hasten into dry leaves and hardened mud.

NOTE

In pre–World War II Martinique, different types of fat would be offered for sale in the open-air markets.

House for the Dead

The molting of monk robes, dry gaping mouths. We, acolytes,
swarthy Cassocks in Roman sandals bathing in sunlight. The redhead
priest
    dustless, drowned by a dream of shade
    or perhaps reminded by his aching toe of Canada
    from whence he came.

Behanzin

He burns, a faded star from the deepest sun; in the mirror of our limestone, his wives scattered about him.

No one knew him O wind. Nor mocked him, praising villainy and chortling at his *kora.*

In the depths of our shackled minds the restored king laughs our lunacies, cries our night, dies our denials.

NOTE

Behanzin: A king of Dahomey, exiled to Martinique.
kora: An African musical instrument.

WHAT BEGINS

Country

    The child does not exist apart from the spherical protuberance, nor
from a globe racked with log struts, the child
    Rotates on his rupture, belly in orbit and flowing with rhymes,
toward this black tumescence
    of the navel.

Iron-dogs

Gray shadows devouring
the daylight's fervor in their vagrancy like a weight
by a block that holds faster than a dream fastened to blistering terror
they fall into the canal
forced by so many
beclawed torments

Letters of Calling

We will not beg, a hand blocks the roads
Scintillating and bridled the stylishly dressed law becomes us
Insect honor of ticket windows
With elytrons spelled out from sweat to blood

Country

Sun
green measure born from a hollow
from the sea's kidney
from intoxication amid the pots we do not have to pee in

into the quartered blue

In Savane Square

He sticks his arms straight out violently
Hails his shadow cast on a stone
Pounds some enemy on the sunlit tin roof
Nails a whole cyclone to him (arms dangling)
Beats him down with broken words
staggers
endlessly closed painless
without eye law or wind

NOTE

Savane Square: The town square in Fort-de-France.

Privileged Prose

He who filters a gold-plated word through the quick of his mind, who knows how the sheep is skewered, who could have taken charge in Africa (having helped the colonies), who chews allamanda mixed with tallow, who is not the Trojans but Hector, who vacations in the Great Capital, who is nigger but universal, who adapts his rank as he goes, in a word, he who has faith in Humanity.

Factory Still

Tortoise
gnawed from a tree tinged with blood
it stirs its transparence on the side of the road
already read there
by ghosts, discount-stored.

Country

I get drunk from a worn-out conch
its red vein lost its color in the iris of its blue vein
I probe it fill it with sand-grains of sadness
(our misfortune is a maritime one sleeping in the noon of beaches)
into the speechless ravage, with all my might
I blow

Moreover

They rend each other's arms to a monotone lament
Since long ago on the mornes this same motion of the machete
Carves countless one-armed men whose
hams
Reek severed future

HIGH WOODLANDS

Prose

When the bovine dream calves only a pile of rosebushes,
leave
only a cry dispersed in star and embers of which too much is written
we pound out language, long fallen into its ravine
like nonsense limping through the mangrove,

more rigid than thorny wood more
insufferable than a yoke.

Dlan

You cry out you meander your weight your side tether you to what you defend on earth you stray you thrust: for how many days gone by flights of years have you bound it amid the commotion of where your bed lies; and this is the sleeping beast at the quick of the beginnings of time's footsteps who cries out
(Dlan Dlan Dlan descends again)

NOTE

Dlan: An abbreviated form of *de l'an,* meaning *from the past;* the name of a character in Glissant's novel *Malemort.*

Dlan

Those who burn their eyes from the smoke of ovens have seen viscera
and gloom: the unknown swelled with foliage before him, dogs picked
up the scent from far behind, the patch of acacias nailed him to the
fresh composted dirt (within the tormenting shocking unsteadiness and
crying out)
 Dlan Dlan Dlan descends again

Dlan

You are seized by the night of ropes up high you cry out you drift witness the tremor the mass, ruptured by so many cries, is illuminated, naked black become dimpled leaf, you stray scarcely daring to set your foot on the capsized burning: as in the early ages, stunned to see his forest made lucid with heat and wind, he descended a maroon filled with antiquity.

The Doubter

When the summit yields to the ease of the valleys, there where shade wears wind-wrecked ferns, what trace is left of the foliage, the ancient woodfoot festering stench that lures and captures?

The Doubter

Master of ropes of bamboo of holes of shade where the odor of
midnight sours.

Earth dresses, begins to burn. But the gripping sea, dries by rocks
amid caned leaves.

But the sea.

Trace

From this instant a dream in which we crawl: from mastiffs hairless in the tumult of acacias of dust to these others from somewhere else who are quiet and adept, sheepdogs with a taste for Vietnamese, wolves who chew on the African

here in a well-deserved respite: do you see, the pact we have made with dogs,

in this morning of distant war we pray that twenty-five years from now they will love us like never before they will never eat us not ever eat us not.

Role

Enticing us to believe that the play emerged from our own desire, that we designate act and denouement in the world: knowing if they take form and fall from the last day's chaos in keeping with comedy or tragedy; or if they paste themselves to a curtain that is never raised, glued to an indistinct earth, itself liquefied.

Ashes

    carnival
of singing instead of summits and satin half-masks instead of full

    hoods straw-cracked where the moon nails you and
vanishing
withered things instead of living ones and organdy instead of sack

    through dead streets of the city, during a night of death or through a
sallow afternoon.

Language

The star grinds out the letter, it is a ballot box. Every no-vote comes out a yes-vote. Mr. Lesprit's secret hoard.

Oh for a rock to throw.

NOTE

Mr. Lesprit: A mayor in Martinique.

Country

In the passageway south of lands. In the morning's salty frost. In the
vigor of clay digging this fate. In the decrepitude of the flat palm of
hands. In the voice of the infinite through deserts and waterspouts.
In an echo with neither wave nor din. In the begging. In a wound deep
within somber greens. In mud unloosing bamboos from cement, and
in a naked old man watching for lightning through the night. In a
dead body uprooted by dredges. In crawling. In a mad driver leaving
behind his sallow tractor. In preciosity. In the mouth of a political and
mendacious fish. In the dread at the heart of stones within your whole
heart. Where all land reaches you.

DEAFER THAN THE SEA

We descend as friends
Shell after shell in skin neither rough nor known
Beyond the living there is firm ground and we go down
Without seeing the trajectory of our essence
Without a hand soldered to the bedrock
Everyone against everyone forever in the
Sailor's scarcely hidden laugh

And deafer than the sea I fired wildly into the fields
Of the One who broke the other story
With the winnowing basket of words
Beyond the knife of potter's earth
Encrusted with stones.

Words of a pompous sailor
visiting, on the run and dead to the world within him
overcome with his own face and how often do you cry out
ah how kind you all are

NOTE

"ah how kind you all are": A reference to De Gaulle's apostrophe to the Martinican people, "Ah qu'êtes-vous français!" which was intended to mean "How French you are" but also incorporates the suggestion of an inquiry—*Êtes-vous français?* or "Are you French?"

MALEMORT (TRAGIC DEATH)

Salt Marshes

When you want only to work or perhaps burrow, stroll stone after stone into the far South. You will see the sad foam unravel at the crag of the Devil's Table.

Country

It is said the wolfsbane carves us into a white wake
Dreams of sand hollow us out of lust
We cry out gray dogs in a half smile
We sit gaping wastelands of us.

Handsome Men

You who have worn defeats you sing of humanity
Pale foliage of absence in the forest and your pollens
Expiring ages ago, you do not see ahead
You bellow about humanity you waste away in the wind
Of your face O transparent ones

Green Ray

Sands gnawed by tedium
We await the jolt of a scintillation
That will lay us out in the wear and tear, to blanch.
We wasp time.

Vaval

through groove and stalk
without a single fire within a single calyx
we burn giants we steep their ash
poetry un-earthenwared

NOTE

Vaval: An enormous Carnival figure parodying some prominent celebrity, which is burned on Ash Wednesday, with its cinders and ashes falling into the sea and the onlookers making a great show of mourning.

Mangroves

The futility of the mangrove is fodder for crabs
There tatters of the dead enfoliate shelters
Plaster and debris produce refugees
All by the side of the runway where it hums.

Poetic

Understand heat time
Rock heat
wedded sorrow
vaporous cry
vowel by vowel
made concrete.

MONOMAGIC

Cactus

Serration of fangs on the windward crest
They obstruct the pollen of time
They illumine the stroke of noon
No one can grasp them
They vanish into the distant past.

In Actuality

When I see us amass flattery on our faces, gather the spewed foam of
the dock: two Bostonians, one from Salento, a lollygagger, all uprooted

I resolve that these factories are naked zombies of the afternoon oh!
how fully we've made ourselves into
   foliose and peculiar tenants.

NOTE

Salento: Capital of the Salentins of ancient Italy.

Study Days

An offering to the manifest Visitor the fat of our teeth, and our hands, palm side up.

Through him we have come to know how the pistil is sweet to the flower: we are thankful.

Should the Arrival deign to speak of us, after drinking, we would love to graft our knowledge to his Noon.

The Alchemist's Fire

He prowls amid waters planting them with transparencies. What vow rends the masts and defoliates the eye? He has sealed an edict of nothingness between two worlds.

You never build in the prow of a rainbow.

Fiefs

   Have you faith
   the way he coils toward the word, where the flame is subdued

   Have you faith the way he gasps out spaces vast as a cargo ship's hold,
saying so little

THAT WHICH OPENS

Ideal

Universals oh universals we exhaust the deserts and coasts we decorate
oil rig isles with flowers
What holy men ship us messages for our kiddies from Roche-Carré
To us the water is thick with hunting blinds with space with our
homes
our bodies.
We have imbibed the latex sap of the past and tomorrow oh we
splatter
Universals

Ball and Chain or Ash

The earth brightens, leaving us through fluid patches. It flees from our breasts, our hands. We flow, nimble in the din. An enemy is uprooting something somewhere, we congregate, we shudder, we swear at one another in unison. Cursing with calm those not here. The absent outmaneuver an army, beyond the mornes. Let us wager that the earth will burst forth in our heads, a thickening.

Strike

Exhausted from watching for the iris they ran away from morning
Nearly falling in their auction of bagged recluses
They strike at the arms: so many one-armed maroons
Guide their hands to the shoulder-stump of an unknown crime.

"Within the Budding Pineapple Groves"

The promised bird of rescue winged them with its opal
They plunged into our voices like wounded pulleys
they hoed
With machetes the field of leaves crowned with blood.

NOTE

The title is a reference to C. K. Scott-Moncrieff's translation of the second volume of Proust's *À la recherche du temps perdu* (*À l'ombre des jeunes filles en fleur/Within a Budding Grove*) and to an obscure novel by Pierre Benoit in which West Indian lovers are described as embracing under the shade of "pineapple trees," which do not exist. (The pineapple, a bromeliad, reaches a height of only a few feet at full maturity.)

Guadeloupe

Let us breathe a sigh of relief our neighbor has rejected its bondage
Oh let us confine privilege to wicker baskets and drosses of freighters
Oh we have done so well to choose the deaf carbuncle it suits us we sigh
with relief our neighbor will grow alone where we sit suspended in
paltry repletion what does freedom matter.

Ones

Within us—the other side of sands—a jolt that cries out yes from the soul to any passerby.

But see—heart of stone—the knot of flame that swallows us and from this cry makes a fire.

Throttle

We had no word that does not come from you. There erosion and
monotony desiccate this taste for departure, making us so.
   We navigate our words into the depths of this winnowing.

Tomorrows

There is no inner world. You will not be able to hide behind your own face.

This is why we should undo this running dry and plunge into so many absences, sinuate until reborn, black in the rock.

DREAM COUNTRY, REAL COUNTRY

to unspeakable wonder
to freedom that blooms on stumps

Country

We raged at your holds the wind peopled
Your high rails for counting the bodies
We spelled our herd of cries from the wind
You who know how to read around the landscape of words
    where we wandered
Detached from us who cry out our blood to you
And on this bridge hail the trace of our feet

Let us sing praise to the foam as well as to the manatees
Spirits of abyss and alluvium how
We uproot the Open and encroach on all that is Unique
You who know how, in our filth and our blood, to bury the writing
In which so many prophetic fissures star into night

An expanse of tar oozes around the sweet grasses
Which is it, this country that strives through seeding and salting
This mild senseless speech, of reddish stars
Between stones of water and green of depths
What are you rending, knotted with flax where thickly foam up
The magnets of the mountains and pure diamonds and what
Word pierces through for you, finds its south

We breathe this country that is drying up inside us, the country
Stretches out from such a dream in which no water makes a sound
Let us shout, "Like the wind, also the past," for this cry
Is broken with sugar, a parable of a mill in this country

We there are overcome as first light
Laughing and about to drown, mud of ravine, born
From another flotation
We spell that we come far away from you where navigates

The Unique, our profound evil. Cutlasses
Melt in the light of workshops. Deepwater crabs
In gray crab-traps torment our thirst
The story in an arc encompasses denial

Some sands crackle. Those who take rank in the sea
Even those who ran from our eyes
Smile back at us sweetly there. We are their Gentiles
We measure the trace of their toes in the wave
We dry them beneath the sea-olive trees

Who has patience in dung and encumbers our musings
Goes up as the sea's blood mixed with rust of ball and chain
We crack the country of the past in the fetter of this country
We moor it to this mangrove that feigns memory
We go back up the stream of exhausted love and discover man and
    woman
Bound together by an iron chain of cleanly forged rings. We laugh
Because we don't know how to tie the *a-tous-maux* and the thick corn
When the earth of yesterday stirs up rocks and itching within us

NOTE

a-tous-maux: See the gloss in "Traces" at the end of this chapter.

The Country of Before

Far away the country rang out. In the plowed clearing
Between the high folds of inscrutable trees
This noise, beaten bronze, fell in grass
We were two, people of night and people of clearing
First country
That we did not know was first
Any more than the wandering sheep knows the river
That tears him with a water like thorns

The door in the middle clad the forest's edge with iron. No foliage
blew in the blue whence the creeping
Withdrew. Walls crumbled beneath the hand, the fingernail
Scratched flooding rivers on them

Did we know that the spur surges deadly at the groan
Of oarstrokes
We know. Being unknown does not dilate the sea
Any unlimited thing disappears at doors
We are born from this sifting of sea water
From the single imperceptible flank of the earth like corn

We run in the crowd having cried out to dogs
Eaten fried cod in the light of burned-down candles, the night
Slips into our flanks cries
Roll in the ravine of the dead
We have no sheets to raise ourselves up on algae
Irremediable and we hail with the agoutis
All the animals that swim in our hearts

Laoka crushes sand instead of millet
And the Enofis stretch out the night into foliage
Red-fingered Milos wrings out bronze beats out swords
His belly shines like a woman about to give birth, Milos
Sends us word, so between the heights of branches rises
Straight up, beneath his hand, our mother the moon

In the troop of children who touch the Blind Man's forehead
Ringing out in force they sing the Ho-a, only one
Trembles up in the tree, casting a shadow on the square
They run the thousand thirty steps, the ochre ramparts
With vultures on their palisades, they have
Armed noon with its root, openhanded
Only one will die from the span of the sea's hand

So do these children turn around the hunting spear
Encounter their age
Disperse naked among the white metal
Suddenly cold with knowledge stumble, they are dry men
So we congeal in memory
Like grease around mouths

For not crowning the song with our stony fingers
Dumb we overflow from the One that fell
Ata-Eli we cry out, born of Enigma and Beast

Blind man whose hand gives the gift of sight
Far away in death the hosanna of boats
Cries out Ata-Eli the naked disgrace of my blindness O All-in-Darkness
This is not to draw around the globe of my pupils
(As a child sticks his finger in the socket and pulls
So that his eye thrusts forward with a tree's groaning)
The patient vegetation of your smile

She, wounded river, watches, cries out in silence
They are wedded by senses we have lost

Time of the humid—singular earth—and of sorghum
The nubile Being devotes its islands to the fire
The Being seated at the prow of earth presides
Astonished, we row till our hands bleed
Bump up against the One sovereign and frail
In the Season our aimless shouting
A tray of words falls down in a pile from dry air
Level with the clay walls

Oh take this transient pleasure and pile it up
Next to the First Wife's garden
Lenten mango-trees have bloomed with dew
The mango melts and is of trembling mint
We crouched sweat frizzing our hair
Having drunk from the cup you call yours, O woman
In your multiplicity we convoked the One
We slept gaping near the pond. O my suffering on your track
Grows the accursed banyan tree. So jousts and speaks
The storyteller Ichneumon

We who are not poets or mad singers speak clearly
Our voice scowls at the folds of the blue mahoganies
Our stories turn clear from turning toward the fan in the evening
Children tell them from one year to the next

There is no connection O storyteller
Between name and earth or wind
And cinders. The depths heaved up
He raises these ocean depths in our pasts and our hungers

Ata-Eli, the Blind Man, and Ichneumon

Fire ho fire
She is dried up and exhausted
Her roots stammer a word
Drifted out on our ravines
She cries out our hurricanes O sails
She announces upon the expanse
A surprised flower a flower
Genipa flower O genipa

She cries out and it's a canna
Listen we beseech her
Do not go near the fire

    When solitude has grown, I invent afflictions so I can soothe them
    Why do you talk that way? Ah I am rambling like a herd of wild
fire-animals
    We will get big in proportion to the aloe, as secret as it is glabrous,
and propitious

Here has chosen the night, leave it
I like the one who cries out in the night he takes
Before him the thing to establish
Here has chosen the fire of the chosen dead
A rush of blood from which rises
Tomorrow more transient than the past

    Do not trouble my rank with this rumor of earth, ah let my daytime
slip away, in friendship for you
    Corolla, we pray you
    Do not go near the fire

You are struck dumb on the lip. What hand can hold you back? From the midst of your destiny to these shores of Transparencies? Immobile in your thunder. In your lightning in your thunder. Oh already dying in this setting sun. Oh immobile already

The high boats move us. The low boats assail us. From the most silent sea, where I go now! Come

The sun sets on the Mountain. Come see the sun bathe in its shadow, and slowly die

Song of Ichneumon

I wandered, in the most angry place. Violet peacocks trembled on our hands. O failure of vision, under the helmets of water willows. I was the one buried alive who navigates upon the numerable river. There was no wind on your face, and your eyes were burning. Today we grieve

Man rejected by tenderness. Like a tamarind tree of the Indies, that dries up. Only this suits him, between the eyes, the ash of an Ancestor who is broken to pieces without a word

Ichneumon sings the hard lament. He does not see Laoka
She commands the Enofis she disarms the Ho-a
He touches the Blind Man's forehead but his eyes do not dare
Now the earth splits. On each side the Unknown
Once as a river to which we laid waste and once
As reality which is inedible

Thus we renounce much more than exhaustion. We are legion deeply rooted in each laugh. We run through the city and dare the sea. The rough sea binds us. I see you deserted, all dressed in our distances

Oh the forests are possible to fire. We follow you, we follow you higher up than the heights of the undergrowth. The roaring of the past lifts us up among you

Earthy water has oozed from their torn fingers. They have kept watch toward the mountains, but the rain of sands did not turn. They ask. Who put this crown upon our heads? This crown of mad suns

Be not the beggars of the Universe
When drumbeats announce the final act

For Laoka

You are the other reason, which makes its way within, where the muds
Are red with our cries and the grease in our hair winks
You are the hidden taste we give to our words
In the night when straw budges and bamboo cracks
You are renunciation, at every sunrise O one renounced
We push you back into the straits of our foreheads you are
Ocean where braced with iron we place
The fragile algae of our breath

In what goes by touched seedbed and exhausts
We pledge our eyes to you
Beaten copper rises to your forehead your ankles praise
You are the woman who navigates, a dead child at the breast
You are, you must be, this people that ascends and its breath
Grows heavy in the ravines where only our footprints grow
You are pride that gives way to the heart when in the town square
Only sand beats us, the sand in which your race is rewritten

Going off on a dream with the young ladies who pound iron
I see what in daylight melts into this palm tree
Daughter of copper, flax of bronze, are you the one transhumed
Who tramples the footprints of the flock and opens space
Of so many such used-up omissions
I constellate the absence you make with my own self
From a bit of wood a little leaf a public auction
My song opens up a displaced madness in the south

You are gentle to the one you banish among himself
Like a too hot sand mixed with sand at midnight
And like the hand of the past that recloses night without a sound
You are gentle to him whom you afflict but who shines

The bell of the flock sounds out over the red grass, the animals
Swarm lumplike in the blue uncertainty
There are gods flying by there, we kill them
The earth crawls to your forehead, crowns you with a burning tree
What is this pain half as tall as the filaos, this sweetness
For which the matting rolls and puts the headrest far from the fire

You spell out how to share the morning and where
To lock up your nudity you denounce the path
Where the fire sings that it creates you
You hurl heart lava torrent of blood riveted
In this cyclone you make

No one knows that the song comes from this fire in which
    copper melts
Milos the red-fingered sings of a light so fragile
Livelier than the moonwater frothing over us
Does he suffer so many deaths in every word
The storyteller puts out before him a mass of animals and aromas
And it is Milos and Ichneumon whose word has unlaced
The suffering of the country of the past
From the broken ravine of this present country

Song of Thael and Matthew

When acacia has adorned her
In water a woman desires herself, she is a branch
Her life calls out on the savanna
An old man with straight skinny legs
Folds up yellowed sheets and arranges them in piles
In the ninth, unsealed wound
The eye of this god fills the past
A plump child with plump legs spread
Between sand and hunger cried out his finger
Two black fish are eviscerated on thirteen rocks
We acquire knowledge of aridity

The bathwater splashes, and the child collapses in the pondwater
where three frogs speak to him. On the injured foot, brush three leaves
of hot mint upon the wound. He sleeps in the blue story, where the leaf
has perspired on his skin. The child, waving beneath the pail

Neither this rock that rigs a rush of words on my forehead
No more than which carpenter carved my bones
Neither which path of lightning-white zombies
I do not know on what earth or what sea

The river and the sea born at the same time
From a single volcano the river the sea
Give us life and take away memory
Air yells at the tin roof like a crazy bird
It decapitates the shadows
We start up our animals
We rummage through the cyclone's mud
Our dreams and broken oaths, our dead woods
A shattered mongoose
There is no water to drink all water

Accumulates there in lovely memory
Lone bull when the only enemy has fallen

Lightning brushes the Mountain
Dominica is far away with its torment
A hundred dead come to us through the clouds
We can glimpse nothing of Grenada O winds
In the clearing of our words
We cry out the One who capsizes inasmuch
Sets fire to us with charivari

Because we are unknown
We flow in this river
Gravel marks the passage of time on sand
A long thing slithers off into bamboo

Among the bulls a zebu keeps watch he nibbles
The smell of grass is blue perhaps he dozes
He makes a flock of what will come
He inseminates truth in the mangrove

And the man who is forest says I am not Ichneumon
Nor am I a tree that makes a spear in the Square
He says What Enofi has run into our soul
What blind man talking took us by the hand
We do not dare that the Ho-a be a prayer to us, seafire

Then the good morning dies where the agouti stands stubborn
Its right paw pierced by a spine
Its eyes have plowed the ridge with a thousand cries
More aghast than grassless memory

Stone cries not thus to rock nor summer for fire
The rock is propped in the heart
We navigate the depths
High up Ata-Eli dreams of soul
There you are unhauled from our ancient wreck
A whole wooden people out of tune from the very first vow

Our ancestors lying all along the spreading grass, carefully
We turn into the country

NOTE

"A long thing": According to tradition, there were originally no snakes on
Martinique. The French colonists imported venomous snakes from Brazil and set
them loose in the forests to flush out escaped slaves. The snake is even today
considered a dreaded enemy by the descendants of slaves, and never named directly,
but only by the circumlocution, *bête longue,* or long beast, long thing.

For Mycea

O earth, if it is earth, O all-illumined into which we have come.
O plunged into the brightness of water and the plowed word. See that
your words have liberated me from this long dream where so much blue
has mixed with so much ochre. And see that I am coming down from
this night, hear

If night puts you down at the height of the sea
Do not offend the sea in you by stranding the old gods
Only flowers know how to scale eternity
We call you wounded land oh how much our time
Will be brief, like water whose bed cannot be seen
Song of water piled upon sad evening water
You are gentle to him you keep from your night
Like a too heavy gravel hidden on the strands of midnight
I have led my oar between the islands I have named you
Far away before you could call me asylum and breath
I named you Unpossessable and All-fleeting
Your laugh separated blue waters from unknown ones

I named you wounded Earth, whose wound is not controllable, and
clothed you in unrooted recitatives from crannies of the past
    Crushing dust and lowering my words to the paddocks and pushing
the mute gray bulls to the edges
    I consecrated you a people of wind where in silence you fall over so
earth you create me
    When you rise up in your color, where is an infinitely enfoliated
crater, visible into the future

I write in you the music of every branch, grave or blue
With our words we illuminate the water that trembles
The same beauty makes us cold
The land has unlaced, blade by blade what yesterday

You bore as cargo on your overflowing river
Your hand calls back this pack of rumors into something new
You are astonished to burn more than old incense

When the noise of the woods is exhausted in our bodies
Amazed we read this wing of earth
Red, in the anchorage of shadow and silence
We take care to collect in the aloe flower
The burn of water in which we dip our hands
You, more faraway than the acoma insane with light
In the woods where it acclaims every sun and me
Who without respite am implacable with this wind
In which I have led the wild past

The water of the mountain is more solemn
In which dreams do not veer
All the green falls down in naked nighttime
What leaf dares its petulance
What birds oar and cry
Thickly hailed from mire my country
Uprooted season which returns to its source
Only a red wind pushes its flower up high
In the swell which has no depth and you
Worn out, unraveled among frangipanis
Where do you get these words you color
With earthy blood swooned on rind
You cry out your fixity to all the accursed country
Is this, O navigatrix, memory

Sadder than the night in which the agouti stops
His right paw pierced by a spine
At break of day he crouches and is determined
He licks the wound and recloses night
So do I lean in over my words and assemble them

Into the windblown place you used to come to lay your head
In this silence to which you consecrated how many celebrations
Your waking your worry your reverie your storms
The covey where you play with the malfini
The blue bursts of time you splashed us with
So the words make me burn mahogany
The ravine where I sleep is a brazier laid out immovable
The day in this night placed the wound that made us

I do not write to surprise you but to do justice to this plenitude of impatience that the wind calls your beauty. Far away, sky of clay and old filth, real
And the water of my words flows, as much as rock arrests it, where I descend river among moons that strut on the bank. There where your smile is the color of sands, your hand more naked than a silent vow

And is no more than ash heaped in brush
Is no more than a bewilderment in which the sky begets
Aloe water does not soothe the timid flower
The stars sing of one gold which is not heard
At the crossroads where the sap was broken on the wheel
To so many who cry out, inspired by the wind
I hail the unexpected wandering
You emerge from the word, and disappear
You are the country of before, given to make amends
Invisible we lead the highway
The earth alone understands

NOTES

acoma (acomat): One of the trees that has disappeared from the Martinican forest. But we should remember it (Édouard Glissant, *Caribbean Discourse,* translated by Michael J. Dash [Charlottesville: University of Virginia Press, 1989]).
malfini: In Haitian Creole, hawk.

Country

There where countries and winds are the same inexhaustible water
Before birds had warped towns and woods
I hung high up this denuded linen, the voice of salt
Like a depthless mud neither diamond nor blue snare

At that span where all lava is amazed to congeal
Becoming being, and being part of pure becoming
There where country and blood were mixed with what was left
I grew up in the armor where the thirteen winds wasted

Ata-Eli old dream of soul and sky
Where the weary storms became enamored of each other
We took our hand from the worn-out alphabet
In the mists of these words the veiled cry, bespattered
The long cry of birds hurled into this sea
And in the seas we have more writing than it seems
Wounded yawls in which the chinks strained

As they were sealing unsalted planks of the forward bridge
The surge of our steps
As they were clinching these final touches in the stern
Here is music of algae and tall ships
The sea, here is the ferrous sea embraced
By so many broken-down piles
Brimful of so many raucous words
Rougher than huts of ochre
Or than cloven masks

The red earth has drunk the earth brought back
The work we are towing is a dream of the sea
We recognized the sesame and the astonished silks

I have this earth for dittany in the morning of the village
Where a child held the forest and towed away the riverbank
Do not be the beggars of the Universe
The mountain creek here recomposed gives us
The luster and ochre of pretemporal savannas

O woman adrift, we raise ourselves up on a propitious surge
You are new in the humus that hailed you
A cave has opened up its family to us
From island to crater there is a burst of waves, blueness
Still and burned field of water like a manchineel tree
I take my earth to wash the old wounds
From a hollow of brine entangled with avowals
But so heavy to carry, O mangroves, so heavy

Traces

Gloss

A-tous-maux: My brother the initiate planted it in front of the house, to ward off cyclones, and so misfortunes would melt and scatter.

Long-beast: Known, at this crossing of the waters, the unnamable wake of the serpent.

Gommier: Tall ship, where wind is frayed on the knife of speed.

Mantou: Alliance of carapace and bristle, violet. A deepwater crab.

Pacala: The most fragile of yams, the most naked, from Guadeloupe in Martinique.

Tre: Tray on which we offer every island, every cake.

Yole: In our seas this is a low boat, which pares away the roundness of time, relentlessly.

Legend

Ata-Eli. In the house that reappeared, she makes merry with sixteen border guards. We fall into her, forgotten.

The Blind Man. In a corner of the Square, like the hunting spear of words.

Les Enofis. These are the Spirits that protect us or sometimes, capriciously, turn away.

Le Ho-a. My friends, every tale we sing is a Ho-a, that is to say, a stone.

Ichneumon. The poet bandages the wound, like the mongoose with the ravaged eyes, broken upon itself.

Laoka. We invent her and adorn her with eminence. Love is ferrous like the forest and the sea.

Milos. First there was the blacksmith. But we have not a single metal left to hearken to.

Real

Mathieu. In the green fire of the forest, you meet your double. If you can, try not to stop.

Mycea. She by whom the poet is enraptured, the one he names at every blowing of wind. But whose words do not explain.

Thael. It was he who raised this baroque song, untranslatable into any language—even the one that gave form to it—and which therefore is suited to any manageable idiom.

FASTES

for the clearings that will delight in such opacity

*Here is allocated to praise a subterranean geography
whose breaches are never erased . . . Here is a remembrance
of seers and those who remain, may they recognize one another . . .*

*My time took hold of their images: countries and woodlands that called
out to me, deserts in which I wandered.*

*This is an offering to them, of suitable language and
obscurity by means of which they disappear into an unexpected wholeness
of word: like a knife that pares ever larger moons from the sculpted skin of
shadows.*

AUGURIES

Assouan

As princes sweep sand from the portal
A lone elephant eclipses the sun
The crowd yells of an imperfect God. Such softness
As a child, delighted, celebrates the water on her face

Gît-le-Coeur

Fallen Destinies devised the chessboard
And Paris has lost the victor's chalice.
It is a marble, it is like Rock, we mesh
La Tarantule with *L'An Deux*, mortality, *L'Ange á Tobie*

Malendure

Fragrance of campeche from the hands' cuts
Tongue of hibiscus, nearly falling into fine saffron.
Word of mangosteen articulated through peats and storms.
Road's twine chokes the ache of a *gommier*

Deux-Choux

Rocks, night-dread, mires, neither sky nor sign
Opaque almond tree spies, a long beast sideways
In the magma where we fall all seas converge
Disasters, deaths, the turbulence, the dray

Lucques

Sacrifice the olive to the wells' rosettes
Joy to the grass snake spied from the path!
And to the ochre, the thistle
Chasm of wanderers thunderstruck stone

Morne des Esses

Suddenly the house leaves the abyss of the mountain
The trembling voice overtakes the descending wind
A passerby runs to the quaking earth, crying out
Innocents play in a shelter of ferns

Great Wall

The fields' slight-fever envelops the last rock
And beyond, Mongolia bereft of thorn and bush
Small passage of sky has cleared a fire of enticements
That watches from the moon and purges burning

Longitudes

"I gave instruction on navigating to Lusitain, of which no one else
      speaks,
We came, mad, from Mälmo, Fez, and Valladolid.
Our dialect, Castilian, spoken by a red-haired preacher-bard.
"I am Irish on one side and Berber on the other, like knees supported by
      chocks."

Erfoud

A tender rock sprays dust
From foliage newly grown each noon!
From the headlights trembling in the heart of fossils,
Let night not withdraw its jetty of sands

1962

How many storms for a sun that thunders
Let the year be a place and the place a malediction!
The one in the distance, his hand dreams, his eyes discern
This quay drifting madly to Saintes, unspeaking

Gorée

Bring down, brothers, bring down the highest storm
We will never arrive at the dazzled attic window
Our bodies will never illumine the black sand
Even so, here, we dream of a bank of effervescence

Calabash

Apocal Babsapin Totol Atiquiliq
Sonderlo Macaron Prisca Godbi, the beloved
Catlike Filacier brandishes his knife at the masses.
Your word blocked the barge, floating there

Avant

Gaping embroidery ice's splinter on the hedges
Singular eye of thistle cropped on the frozen shrubs
Bend down, careful of the attic's beam
Words of the time-driver braise in the hearth

Quebec

Leap, as in the *o* from *oti ou yé*
High and strong in the fading season
To push ahead, where the poles weaken
The brazen new horse

Falls

From the densest recesses the foam congeals
We keep ourselves in madness scattered thickly
With time to bind the place, the spear, the memories of water.
When we wake, the sun sleeps

Eget

The same noon opens this garden,
We were distant
Like eagle or hawk.
The sea a bed of diamonds

Chapelle Saint-Jacques

I named the singer and his piano as target
The Turkish paintings, the philosopher and Aucassin,
I neither surprise the grated shadow of the vaults
Nor the plasters that unleaf themselves from a bitter abyss

Bezaudin

Past the river rocks
Faded beyond recollection
A defiant mule hauls a nameless man
The veranda sails, the seated man cries out

Puerto La Cruz

The one who dreams of fusion becomes a green flame
Porcelain rose has folded its trills into the setting sun
Too much light between two sockets, too much grace
From an ebony tree to a palm tree, slow and sober

La Palun

"This mule knows the way back
Bridle and saddle are rightfully mine
I threw out too much dead sun, soaked with water
In the mill where you watch for the number of Gold"

Tremiti

A blade of grass drifted on the table where we suppose
This solitary horse is from a broken herd
Ashen sea urchins sparkle, prisoners of their own will,
Phosphorescent cornice on the Cave-of-Poets

Oran

Seek, Salah, no more in the Belvedere
The steps cry out the street, what threatens is slow
Secret mission and special passports cannot be hidden from the wind
Let us spread out our laundry to dry and whiten upon the desert

Conchs

The open palm illuminates speeches, conchs, and wood
It capsizes the thefts of mountain and valley
The word for fire is as simple as a droplet endured
The drum so old that its rumble flashes

Lindos

Earth undulates, darkened
The diviner's feet fold
The prophet of stumbling images
The blue disks are in fact bare

Grand Riviere

Throughout, the northern wind herds these rivers
Within every breeze a crater where only flax stirred
Water predictably crowning the muskeg; in the distance
Cree night shivers from the Inuit day

Habana

The young girl cuts ten years to twenty
Her gardens are hailed by blind palms
At the boat's black side, the shrill shooting of lianas
How to get back to this sand, how to get back

Igloolik

So distant in the silence discovered his hand
Shook his hand coated with gizzards and skins
Watched the dogs eating in their pens, while from the frozen bays
The leftover meat and the short day returned to a dry place

Young Camps

On the savanna, cut, cut the ebony Ardennes
His poignant story consumed hunger
Zocli pété konba épi Térèse
Pou an graté kan'nari ayayaï

Skopje

Prophecize that I arrive at the summit before this wind sounds
I have a distinct memory of an abacus that would not turn over
The trout in its haul is more than a short-lived dream
Where the glacier is spoken and the heat is awed

Terres Sainville

–Tornadoes hail the equidistance
–Chaotic huts scatter on pure mud
–The Latin teacher lies prostrate in white alpaca
–A girl shouts at the canal's surges

Teotihuacan

As quick as a summit in the sky such a memory keeps watch
The salting trembles in vain, you do not begin the name
Mouths, familiar words, countries that hasten . . .
The descent is a laugh and the photo is extinguished

Blondel Grocery

In a trembling vertigo of husked peppers on display
Birds of prayer, Indians cloyed in embers
Fleeing the cold and ravenous, sucking mouth to mouth
The spicy breath of milk's passage

Furstemberg

Where are you, who released me from solitude
Where the parting, the becoming, the marching mad
Harpies sleep to a paean!
Their flocks claw new walls, in dense countries

Wounds

Epini, acacia, minutiae of bark that plies
Rock in its day, sweating beast, broken feather
That make skin gray, night's eye, and the wind of a tragic death
With dry legs infinite as truth's wand

Ibadan

The night arms its candlelight
Murmuring blues the frontiers
Look, the Ibos embrace death

I'll toast you ten thousand times
If, without trembling, you lift
The rusted post of the prophet Congo

Suburb in Snow

From the garden station the surveyor refuses to love
What he puts in the grove, white like an alpaca
Wash the layer, so as to efface vanity
This night is too heavy to praise, O wind

Pointe des Chateaux

The ice's water stripped the bark's marble
Where the wind places its tuft and drives its trembling fires
What is unchanging is praised in the sea, molted in rock
Like a child stirring a manioc in his broken froth

Vernazza

The breaking read the highest rocks
Drowning we change ourselves three times in the same night
The small boats in the square yield sun and corridor
Above, the commander's tower is destroyed suddenly

Baton Rouge

They wait for me, there where the rain is open
And the ink in its register sealed nothing but a cry
They wait for me, the plain of grass exalts the altitude
These are friends whom so much sun has deprived

Pont Autou

Galena, Rose-Cross or limestone that turns
Into midnight where light defends itself with cries
Horses and wasps make way for writing
In the bath of the valley, honor! a path devours its shadow

Djobeur

"I have my population of gossips that linger
The helping hands bind up and the breadfruit soups are breathless
The weak coffee and fights peel away like stiff hives
The new arrivals, the laghias and vulvas triumph"

Lieu-Dit

Skin at the auction of the sea soil
Voice that traverses and plants a deaf tree
The red rock, the sparrow hawk, volcano's water
That whirl at Lamentin in the mangroves trees

Rabat

The fiendish wind barked at the metal
Its white sun had neither torrents nor wounds
Every afternoon a leaf held itself
Grounded, to a cliff

Norman

From the moon, absent, even from the bitter pollen
Estonian wind, tree of the past, and maple wine, pure
From the eyelash where the sky spirals a tide spins
Daring only salt and the sea's wish, nothing moving but walls

The Union Road

With you Xamana the best of its word
An eight-year-old tear covers the voice in secret
It is silence in the song that you tame
It is the face of a brother shattered without supplication

Lézarde

Leeches! who make a cry run through the yellowed water
The siren's roughcast splashes, flowing
Too much grass invades the memory
The past shines a headlight on so many dead pigeons

Rowan Oak

We hide in your planks our everyday retreat
You have elected us to the guarded stalls of ants
There were pine cones among the fat leaves
Finally, we dared to address the reluctant tomb in familiar terms

More True Than Day

In Petersburg, one midnight, in a surplice-less snow
The streetlights died away; in their wake
A team of horses fled the past. The Queen returned.
A beggar insulted her, whom a rose adored

The Permanent Part

I send back this fine piquancy
To him who asked, "Will the storm fly away like a clever nigger?"
The answer is: "Every gruel has its inside out
Every dream its crowd, every century its hundred drinks."

Gavarnie

Thirty horses ford and dazzle us
The broken branch inaugurates a theater of water
We are happy to get the part of crowd and people
When we descend, our heads aflame

The Unnamable

The inflamed eyes the eyes
Burn around you
Death in parchment
Sketches bones one by one

Rue Leonce-Bayardin

"You're wrong," she said, "I never hit you
Unless it was in the mangroves where you strayed."
Mother, you cast upon this straying a cold water of fear
The memory of it gushes from every gutter, far into the night

Les Vigneaux

A star rallied the archipelago like *cachiman*
Our islands scatter their acknowledged centuries
Aloud, for once, the garden basks
Only the telescope confides its sky to the waves

Cathedral of Salt

The words that delivered the architrave were silent
In layers, your language irrigates, extends
The depth resumes beneath the hand
The splendors of the truth, madwomen, ensconced in nests

Kinskof

Listen in the assault the rank sea spray of the streets below
Has struck us, frightened us in death
At every summit gape rocks that wind does not arrest
Let us gather other places, meditate upon the year, open up the cold

Caipirinha

Neither have you surprised the venom in the sap
Nor the ball and chain that engaged the green depths
Nor the blood that fled in the short passages
On the sand animated by the slope of the vezou

Cities Angle

The train, gagged with burned linen.
These palms, this sheet of the dead, this day
Where, unable to finish with the year and the leaf
We remained in the sacred gap of Tokyoto

Panarea

Our days are swayed by salinities that number
The sea in the hand, the fires on the heights
And the nights! Oh the nights. They spell to life
The volcano's groan, the only broken story

Caulincourt

What was at the window and rhymed with the enamel
What was that supernatural hunger? What was the elm?
Beauty grew old like scales
Palettes and aromas climbed up to the seventh floor

Cargese

Those who went away dined reluctantly
September has been dead for two moons on your hand
Sea rock is attached to the impossible boat
The poet smitten with fruits turns away from Atala

Prometheus

Near an injured banyan we shall consecrate to the storyteller
His broken word marked the shade of three lagoons
He said he said, "My heart holds but a riot."
The dinner guests crowned the water of his cry in fame

Chavin

The god drowns! The sludge navigates underground
The god shoots his brow at the friezes we pillage
Corn climbs horizontal, on the side of a rock it flows.
The womb dies, the rain retreats alone.

Dragon

From afar, from so far away, from the most secret place this side of the
    new year
Ephemeral, votive, covering the fashionable clothes
That dream, hatch, and coil in nets of heavy paintings
And play back a dream born at Amiens

PAEAN

Paean

At our marine feasts the Americas play palaver
Stories, country and city resonate with this cry!
Holding out arms, we feel sea, sifting on the other shore
Where thickness of age and yellow mangrove hail one other.

Four Ways

Rivers, you drift from succulence to equity!
The ancient food praises complicity with basil
You threw the naked migrant on the sand without seeing him.
The trace of his gods vague in him like poetry!

NOTES

Fastes: Fasti, Ovid's poetical calendar (circa 8 AD) of the Roman year, with its various observances and festivals, written in elegiacs; "fasti: name given to the old Roman calendar which originally indicated *dies fasti* and the *nefasti,* the days on which it was or was not permissible to transact legal and public business" (from the *Oxford Companion to Classical Literature,* ed. M. C. Howatson [Oxford: Oxford University Press, 1989]).

Assouan: Town in Egypt, along the Nile.

Gît-le-Coeur and L'Ange á Tobie: References to "Poème á l'étrangère" by Saint-John Perse, as well as to Glissant's having played a game of chess on the street Gît-le-Coeur with writers Maurice Roche, Jean Paris, and Roger Giroux while reading the manuscripts *La Tarantule* and *L'An Deux.*

Malendure: A place in Guadeloupe that is said to be settled by *maroons,* or escaped slaves. Campeche is a prickly plant with no flowers. The *gommier* is a tropical tree as well as a fishing boat.

Deux-Choux: Route intersected by Tracée and route Saint-Denis in Martinique where the poet spent a night lost in the tropical forest.

Lucques: Town in the Tuscany region of Italy, famous for its olive oil, where the painter Sandro Somare lives.

Morne des Esses: Mountain in Martinique where the poet was caught in an earthquake with his children.

Malmö: City and port in southern Sweden.

Fez: City in northern Morocco.

Valladolid: City in northwestern Spain.

Erfoud: One of the villages in Tafilalt, Morocco's largest Saharan oasis.

1962: The year of Paul Niger's death in an airplane accident in Guadeloupe.

Saintes: Islet in the French Antilles.

Gorée: "Island off Senegal, where slaves were loaded after being seized on the African continent. We all dream of Gorée, as one dreams of a motherland from which one has been excluded: without really realizing it" (Édouard Glissant, *Caribbean Discourse,* translated by Michael J. Dash [Charlottesville: University of Virginia Press, 1989]).

Calabash: A running or climbing plant of the gourd family, native to the Old World tropics; also a reference to Place Calebassier, a meeting place for the poet and his friends.

Apocal Babsapin Totol Atiquiliq Sonderlo Macaron Prisca Godbi: nicknames of the poet's childhood friends; "Godbi" refers to the poet himself.

Filacier: A bandit with whom they frequently associated.

Avant: A commune in France where the poet Jean Grosjean lives.

oti ou yé: Où êtes-vous, a reference to Joual, a fading dialect of the Quebecois; "the horse refers to *Joal:* from *cheval* (horse); designates the French spoken by the urban poor in parts of Montreal and its industrial suburbs" (Michael J. Dash note in Glissant, *Caribbean Discourse*).

Eget: Village in the Pyrenees.

Chapelle Saint-Jacques: A pension located inside an old chapel on Rue Saint Jacques in Paris.

Bezaudin: Mountain near Saint Marie in Martinique, also the poet's birthplace.

Puerto La Cruz: City in northeastern Venezuela, along the Caribbean Sea, where one leaves for the island of Margarita. The porcelain rose is a sculptural flower.

La Palun: Sugar plantation near Ducos in Martinique, where a slave-driver refused to do an extremely difficult task and dismounted his mule, but kept its bridle and saddle, a forbidden act in front of the *béké* (a Caribbean term for white colonists).

Tremiti: Island in the Adriatic sea, where Mussolini sent political prisoners.

Oran: Algerian port on the Mediterranean; there the poet went by the name Salah.

Lindos: Town on the eastern coast of Rhodes.

Grand Riviere: North of Baffin, near the North Pole. Muskeg is a wet forest. Cree and Inuit are the native people of that region.

Igloolik: Inuit camp in Baffin. Both the meat and the dogs are kept outside in subzero temperatures.

Young Camps: The poet stayed in a camp during World War II. Ardennes is an allusion to the novel *Le Village pathétique* by André Dhôtel.

Zocli pété . . . : Creole phrase meaning "Zocli fought with Therese for the last dregs in the pot."

Skopje: Capital of Macedonia.

Terres Sainville: Neighborhood in Fort de France, Martinique, where the poet attended school as a young man.

Teotihuacan: Immense religious metropolis in Mexico during the pre-Columbian era, with temples of the sun and the moon.

Furstemberg: Place Furstemberg in Paris.

paean: Hymn in honor of Apollo or a war song.

Ibadan: Town in Nigeria.

Ibos: Tribe from the eastern region of Nigeria, involved in a bloody civil war with the Angas, a northeastern tribe.

Pointe des Chateaux: Famous monument found in Guadeloupe.

manioc: A tuber, known in granular form as tapioca.

Vernazza: One of the five towns that form the famous Cinque Terre in Italy.

Pont Autou: Town in Normandy, home of the artist Jean-Jacques Lebel.

Galena: Primary material in lead.

Djobeur: "From English *job;* those who subsist by doing odd jobs, in particular by recycling used materials" (Dash note in Glissant, *Caribbean Discourse*).

laghias (damier): "Dance taking the form of a fight. The two dancers are in a circle of spectators, around a drum. The same dance is found in Brazil. The *laghia* is no doubt a ritual derived from initiation. There is always a 'major' (a champion) and a challenger. An exercise in regression. The *laghia* became linked to the production of sugar cane. See also notes in *Great Chaoses*" (Glissant, *Caribbean Discourse*).

Lamentin: Town in Martinique.

Rabat: Capital of Morocco.

Norman: Remote town in Oklahoma.

Union Road: A road in Martinique where the poet once lived and where his brother suffered a serious facial injury.

Xamana: Tree native to Martinique.

Lézarde: A reference to the river in Martinique (the author also has a novel entitled *La Lézarde*).

Rowan Oak: William Faulkner's home in Oxford, Mississippi.

The Queen returned: A reference to the Queen of Spades, from a passage in Pushkin.

beggar: An allusion to Dostoyevsky.

Gavarnie: Community in the high Pyrenees.

Rue Leonce-Bayardin: Street where the poet's mother lived.

Les Vigneaux: Saint-John Perse's home near Toulons.

cachiman: An edible fruit common in the West Indies.

Cathedral of Salt: Underground cathedral sculpted in a salt mine near Bogota.

Kinskof: Residential district above Port au Prince, Haiti.

Caipirinha: Famous Brazilian drink.

vezou: Black juice made from sugar cane that is burned before being distilled.

Panarea: One of the Eolie Islands in the Tyrrhenian Sea, off the north coast of Sicily, Italy.

Caulincourt: Rue Caulincourt, no. 11, Paris, where the poet lived in the 1950s.

Cargese: Town in Corsica where the poet spent some time stranded with very little money.

Prometheus: A poem in honor of Tchicaya U'Tamsi, a Congo poet.

Chavin: Archaeological site of a culture developed between 1500 and 300 BC in the Peruvian Andes.

Dragon: A street once known for art galleries, now known for its fashionable shops.

Amiens: A reference to the poet Paul Mayer, who once lived there.

palaver: Conference with a tribal chief or among tribes.

THE GREAT CHAOSES

Bayou

Off the Meschacebe, Father of Waters. The landscape, vertiginously horizontal, follows the course of the Atchafalaya River. It meets the one obstinate in heights and depths which in Martinique goes from Balata to Mount Pelée, by way of the Trace. Near to a primordial time, water and earth intermingled, in which the rhythm of voice is elemental: Here, measured in eight cadences. Everything melts into this sea and this earth: Mythology, the African night, the imaginary Vesuvius, the caribou of the North. The echo-world speaks indistinctly. The language of the island promises to harmonize with that of the continent, the archipelagic with dense spread-out prose. A disarticulated song in rigid stones, on the trace that leads from story to poem. Thus: "Boutou," baton of death, commander's instrument. "Grand-degorge," the native Caribbean who threw himself with all his own off a cliff, refusing Occupation . . . The lilies die, a fertile decomposition, by the grace of vanished deities. Commemoration of this water. Seizure of avenues.

Let the wild lilies be reborn
The upriver gods too, reborn
True gods, true hordes the Saturn
Ogoun, the sirens, the lilies

The sagacious sea came in there
And leveled the surface, it has
Opened its valley among the brush
Likened suffering and headpiece

The remains of day close up
In a bank of water beneath a sluice
A man jousts at this work
Like a decimated parentalia

The mustangs were from Spain
And from Peru the sea so close
Wait for the year to inscribe itself there
On a rose that does not reproduce itself

What, omen of abandonment
The rumor which is exhausted down there
In the knot of the branch where ennui takes hold
Slowly shriveled

The basket of mastic-trees extends
From Causeway to Gulf, day
Has put its water into clear night
And is reflected there in a Sererean night

Everything tends to silence and regales
With the uncertainty of Vesuvians
A caribou not finished by wind
An expenditure of holly which does not heave back

Which one, omen of untying
The nest where words are trapped like fish
Turbulence mob knotted
In a fault line which is sinking

Where go the apt sorceries
That ride sap into fruit
Where, the bindings of earth
The sprays of air become irrational

Expect only outright failure
Among the ideas that fall from the Shadows
hat pushes far ahead
The golden straw into hard white rum

It only lacks a display of tears
Wild lilies or horde on a high mountain
Lacks only alarm and tawny dearth
And that the oar surge deeply

Only a car falls and rises
The one that navigates through an insane country
Measuring the water of words
By the sound of your gurgling

And comes back to a frail cadence
At the scorching risk of its mornings
The multitudes flee in a stampede
And the birds are bruised there

Level with the May salt, *cayali*
Which fastened star onto noon
Its clairvoyance has a crazy pen
It drowned in miswriting

Of shade, hardened wood, *sugar-bird*
Name of a cry more than of anything sweet
Upon all unfinished roads
We have left its forfeiture.

Ortolan whose song we represent as
Zortolan blessed Zortolan
Their cloud perished, their wind
Became an accursed antiwind

We cry out: This is a piece of earth
On a Vessel from paradise,
Pipiri, tuft which is finished
Where the heights of night take fright

Frigate bird, ah frigate bird, ship
Which is neither yole nor blue clipper
Your feather like flowers
No longer adorn the gray sea urchins

Birds game all gone
Where did they go
Flambants, messengers, turtledoves
So many lives have dried up there

Until from now on
The leaf streams in the mud
The root of water raises liana
To the tree whose fruit is the island

All came at the burned skin of a scale
Sung by the xamana trees
The earth did not dare set oar
To Atchafalaya's heart

Lost gods, looking for work
In separating earth and sky
When water hoots at thicket of foliage
Its yellow clamor, its club

The Enemy hangs from the branch
Indistinctly shriveled
North and south immolate themselves
In its mauve crucifixion

Island words continental words
Congest the same path like brush
A false willow comes dawdling over
To chat up a slow tamarind

What is more horizontal
Than an unmoored savanna
Than a marriage coming undone
Mounts the three feet of a horse

Beles Boutous Mont-a-Missie
Unambiguously assured
Cliff of wind, Great scoured
Squall that tears

Bele, beautiful air and beautiful oath
Of poem turning into tale
And whose rhythm does not misstrike
The swamp's flat prose

Fale, cliff of armpits
So ravined by sweat
We are certain only of wind
Let us trace only the leash of the stick

Let us trace out words deviated
In eight drums of great age
Words that make men dig in the mud
And may the country pull patience taut

The sea goes back to so much childhood
It has cried out its eyes it has
set out bushes in Bezaudin
Squared sand and insane oozes

Gods that let hoes stream forth
Shops laid out drowned beside the road
That hooked the mangroves
To the epiphytes of the bayou

And let die the wild lilies
Beneath the wood pigeons of Balata,
The Trace mixes within its cloud
The water razing the commotion below.

NOTES

Ogoun: Voudou god of war.

parentalia: "Among the ancient Romans, periodical observances in honour of dead parents or relations" *(Oxford English Dictionary).*

Sererean: A reference to the Serere people of Senegal.

cayali: See "Note" at the end of *The Great Chaoses.*

sugar-bird: See "Note" at the end of *The Great Chaoses.*

Ortolan: See "Note" at the end of *The Great Chaoses.*

Pipiri: See "Note" at the end of *The Great Chaoses.*

Frigate bird: See "Note" at the end of *The Great Chaoses.*

Bezaudin: Birthplace of Glissant.

The Great Chaoses

for Sylvie

    Not far from the Seine, in the melancholy vicinity of the Place
Furstemberg and the Buci market in Paris, are the magi of distress, the
homeless, fallen from the horizon. Inflict no romanticism on their exposure,
rather remind yourself that they manifest the world. They are assigned here,
where they try to maraud to some effect. Everywhere an obsession with
vegetables and food. History has debated them and dumped them here.
But along with the unfurled language of their vagrancy. They deflect the
sufficient reason of the languages they use, and this is accomplished by the
opposites of ode or of harmony: disodes. They understand the chaos-world
instinctively. Even when they affect, to the point of parody, the words of the
Other. Their dialogues are all allegorical. Mad preciosities, unknown science,
baroque idioms of these Great Chaoses. Come from everywhere, they decenter
the known. Vagrant and offended, they teach. What voices are debating
there, announcing every possible language?

Magi go forth, who chew grass and soya . . .

In trays sours the precipitude of six mangoes that no one wants
In their firmament, blind edict, they have placed
The disasters the dead, turbulence cartage
Of Earth which rises up in their auction.

Like soap tired of mixing with itself
A bit of froth in these drains made memory
When the pavements attend to the benches they have named.

Having lunated our equipment
Phantasm undulated to us, raised onto the scorching highways
By what sun, which dared not trespass the hole of any yam?
O ungiven, O improbable lakes.

From Bonaparte to the thatch of the Quai des Augustins,
Someone says, "They're convicts!" They say, "It's the earth
Commingling its swell with the people who live here."
And many have stomped the Islands,
Many have stomped out their own exhaustion.

One who brings back to himself all the neighboring chaos
Turning it into his cay, his pallet,
Giving himself to the pile given to him, on hives of bees!
When you repeat your eulogies before his famished mouth.

Storyteller he drags his boat through your boilers,
Cane-cutter in Malendure, he summoned
A paring and three dregs of water from the Fountain.
And then he went to the Orient.

These lines of nothing traced on the earth,
Where space exerts itself in muddy transparency,
These thinkers of thoughts that blow like wind
That ensconce themselves in the cool air,
Their memory is crowned with a simple feather, these gilded places
Low on the wall where nothing is left, not even a sprout or a vegetal scrap.

As though of untanned ivory,
Like a hoe sword . . .

He who rummages in absence has stirred sweet equity
A dipper made from a gourd, a scratched carafe
He who climbs to the Mountain's auction, spins on the sea
He by whom everything has spun

Have they broken the shackle where a frigate lies in the surge
Have they bonded the stone to the knife that cuts the stone's thickness
Or perhaps their bodies would not grow the distance,
Or choked the Story where the beast dreamed pittance?

Or have they not wandered away from their hurricanes
Being neither kings nor those who take aim
Having neither younger face, wooden shoes, nor capstans
Deducing not even from a hoecake . . .

The hour has already scattered.
A swarm a recrudescence, now that the unperceived blows.
So much insipidness in these eyelids, so much emotion
Worn out from the sole burden of a single famished thought.
What is coming is only dawn for you, the exhausted.

The old stage has swept the greenery away
The water of depths resifts water dripping from the roof
Even unto its lair washed with repercussions.

Already old nuisances have let down their rags
The thick straw taken hold in words
Roll, History, turn, riot!
O afflicted.

I shall not take up iron for you nor run with the pack!
But his knee woos a blue cress in the greasy scupper
And he puts together some words and teaches
A gourd naked from drying out before it was ripe
And says, "Where the water comes from, there is the festival.
Where the halter, there goes the beast . . ."

Understanding the broken word.

Disode

> *One that foments in Furstemberg, where the equity pleases us, two
> benches in propitious balance.
> Forgotten in his bay, or tied to a bench—the bench itself uprooted,*

Who, lacerated with clothing, cries out his rades
—Re-avenge this death.

Dying being born, in which his voice boasted—may it make haste
In memory of down-there, when the depths poured water,
Who rose up in sulfur, born of a chadron,
—He reanimates this frozen knell.

One who flaws new beggarhood, execration on every bold thing, saying
"Who speaks in the rain has a lot to say . . ."—Ah! What good is the
tolling church bell, flat from the bottom up like a gone tornado
—Break the law, they undo the rhythm!

Passerby, have only chaos
You disinhaled the flesh of words
Leaving no crumb but bone . . .

Like a sword sword.

"I choose in the scupper, I reach out only to your dissonance. My misfortune pours not therein, it is not the world's screech owl. Mouthful of desert nor bombarded memory.

"Piled up advantage frowns pittance and meaning. The markets converge rudely, I spy blood in them. My misfortune no longer frightens, when the thought of the sewer has annexed disheveled death."

In the tired watering, in the Rue de l'Abbaye,
He ciphers night and makes a sluice of his voice.

This thin breath of poem unswelling
In the river-water where its face drank in the depths . . .

The Passerby says: "This is a learned man! Or a zombie,
But not a madman"—he consults impure onions,

He stakes his memory on this prophecy, his feet
Frozen by rags that scatter like straw, by dislocated fruit-cores.

Darkening the rhythm, he has designated the Great Chaoses
Sap-woman, like-it-men, checkers, Pilles
Come to die at the Petit-paves, in the public square.
These are the silenced Ramnes of your populace! O juices

Black juices
Of disheveled black bay trees.

The Great Chaoses are in the Square! Also the *Kafirs*
The *Bectres* the *Pelées* the *Cinnabars* the *Maronis*
The *Astrides* and *Saramancas, Gros-Morne* people
Mad Austrasians, the seven winter-residents of Eget, Runaway slaves
From old clouds in Australia,
Nomads on ice floes and sedentary types from all over Ethiopia
Alone silenced, at your knees disassembled.

The Great Chaoses have arrived. One who engenders his silence
In rain of sand and does not start, having already begun, at Paracas,
the torture of the god who remade the world four times.
He is adept at imitating, upholds the virtue of redundance: as soon as
we speak of comic opera!
He declaims: "Singing woman. And a man who answers her!"
And he invokes: *"Ah je mange, ah je mange,"* and he shines
In the Godhead of Waters, Yemanja, born upon Death,
Who fought the Anaconda.

The latter did not rise from Amazonia, nor polish any thistle.

Hear the rattling noise her unbandeleted ankles drill in the dew.
She has breathed in too much Oriental space, too much stupor has
imbibed her face,
Do not try to steal from her forehead this lily sealed with fire from a
perfuming pan,

Too much surge is her cry. Too much gaping-open, her race.

And it is only an alga that makes her real and nourishes her for long.

Dialogue of the Great Chaoses

—Have you noticed how many all around are staring at us?
—It's because we're hungry, we feel thirst. This makes us look intelligent.

—But have you noticed how intelligent people don't talk when they eat?

—Ho! I am quite comfortable and happy. I have no more credit
whatsoever.

—A Big Store have I in my country, full of silk goods
Of high fashion in season, newt's liver, jelly,
Fruit of the vine in compote, raw caprine's milk
And precious venison. I have a big Store in my country!
Forty Malmaisons in my country of nail-beds.

And Yet Another Shouted Dialogue

Passerby, O tautologue, you who pass
Through History who slough fodder upon this Market
Who make no deals with those you do not like
Who do not spice your words at auction
Who has never been corrupted by any cry in an accent other than
your own
O Repeater,
Behold the horde in which your prime places us.

Like a hoe that has never hoed.

When the latter has been on intimate terms with his beggar's wallet,
in the four swings of the church
And the Buci market wanders in the middle of the Toufaille
plantation. He says "Sherry"
For cherry, and pronounces: "Should it have been necessary that I
should go, or that I should have been going?"
Toward the undone crabs he feigns new devotion
Risks his hand in false agreement,
"Are these then pincerbeasts?"

Are these marshes and brambles, low weddings
Disappeared from so many accursed winnowings
Pumice words, thumb-piece words to which wind does not harken,
Failed! Are they ravines, nude breaths
In which we mill grain, or protract
Noon heavier than headwind? Could it be
The winged firing in his brain placed
Where wind is winnow, sickbed, fire of water-willow
Crab transformed into pincerbeast
Whose hand cramps and reveals the outline of time?
"Are these then? Are they?"—he says, in his idiom of the flayed.

Renters of old Mondays' butcher-stalls now deserts of soot,
The holy oil that burns them has left neither scales nor must,
Water of the depths has joined the hard water and the evidence
And sprouted a crest of dead-raisin roux.

Men of little rain!
They are the crowd of boiling dullness,
The horizon that does not dance
And the Court that sleeps while the story is told.

They uphold recitation of their defeats,
Language for dodging, and a lot of words for the elemi
And another tongue as well

For the very old Knowledge that has reappeared,
And underrated eloquence for heaving back into the future.

They have their speech put in very Punic dialect
They cry out a flamboyance which is unknown—and likewise for
him—meaning
A scrupulous crab who wanders far from a rank
Leech. A wasp who sorts skies that clouds chew like tobacco.
A flamboyance. Shoots. A redundant cane syrup. And him,

In Furstemberg, where the morning proceeds
With the heat of an ash tree and cool sweet grass,
Lightly touching a creek rendered sticky by starch,
"Are these islands?" . . . he sings—These are upstream

Magi who go forth, chewing the clay of their fingers.

NOTES

the fountain: A reference to the poetry of Charles d'Orléans and François Villon:
"Je meurs de soif auprès de la fontaine."
neither kings nor those who take aim: A reference to Arthur Rimbaud's poem
"Le Bateau ivre."
chadron: See "Note" at the end of *The Great Chaoses.*
Ramnes: A deity of ancient Egypt.
Malmaisons: The house of the Empress Josephine, wife of Napoleon I (divorced by
him in 1809), who was born in Martinique.
the Toufaille plantation: A plantation in Martinique belonging to the fictional Targin
family in Glissant's novel *Le Quatrième Siècle.*

The Stolen Eye

to Jean-Jacques Lebel, Nilotic

The Nile, river of time. Lesson of the Kom-Ombo Temple, where most esteemed is that surgery struck in stone, designating its instruments and its ritual, which serves to restore to the god Horus his eye, no less ritually enucleated by another god. Images of the eye walking or pouring out a tear as wake. The language of water can only be perceived as echo, brisk as a sheet of tin. Stone cartouches give up their secret matter. The moldy smell of words gathered or proffered by the visitor, pile up in real distances: This is the acoma, majestic tree of the tropical forest; or the laghia, Antillean dance which takes the form of combat, revealing harmony and variation. The two languages escape from each other, the one divined in this navigation, the other born with difficulty at the poem's command. A waterless sluice cuts off the flow and the drift, sends it toward the Delta. But in the assumption of the world's news, the two landscapes, Nilotic and insular, faraway, touch and understand each other. Ichneumon and Laoka are again reconciled, to celebrate the restored vision of the god.

The news of the Moon has not violated the hypostyles and the dust of our feet scarcely imprints the sand . . .

At the wind's turning, this projection of progress!
Fern betrampled by cries, appearing and dying . . .
A spirit clings desperately to its sail, which slips away,
a crouching man purifies his hands in an imploring gesture,
—the river dreams, its passages hail us in the crossing.

"My beloved body my beloved body," says the moon to its blue-
oscillated shadow,
"grant the pilgrim nourishment by indirect fire,"
the poem has restrained the fleshes
alloted yesterday in Nilic swell
and which at heart bore silt.

The stolen eye comes to crime!
The lapse of years to us seemed eternal,
nothing remains of so many words but a stripped, demented mass.

The slope of words slides, so simple that in the swell of palm trees,
a water we do not taste, and we exhaust all of it,
by the thirst that within us steals its graves,
by the avid wing of the ibis, and the salinity of sails . . .

And for us thousands of gods roam the world,
when the water of banks scarcely rises,
scarcely descends into childhood . . .

The ibis was spoken. Let the blue birds of Aswan come down there!
These Niles were spoken, in which our baggage rigged bowls of
sand . . .

On the passage that navigates is an enclosure where rivulets
intertwine,
the mind that watches is a dancer, drunk on his worn-out hands.

The news of the world to infinity has struck the stone!

Pass by the great column, their light has praised our brows
placing the bee-with-the-liquid-feet upon the disenlaced reed.

This smoking language, here we pass through it, like rough steel
drowned in echoes!

As the echo rides the metallic ray and which trembles.
—The tree, betrayed, covers its roots with sacred honey.

So does the gush in the distance rally the rock . . .

In bronze fires he sniffs the surface of the water, designates a
stopping-place
we rest in the immobility of fruit, we stammer
a girl-child visits us, black cheeks of untired supplication.

"My beloved body my beloved body," sighs dawn of the boat, "teach them
 the incense of mimosas, the smell of ink," and by a look throws it, drives it
 into the fire of a crippled potter.

Now it is nighttime, the day's progress has set down its hive in silence.
A star sketches its old dream in aquavive
Shards half burn.

Let's go! On the way!—¡Vaya!—And all these languages which bind the dust!

The stolen eye has followed us, where the water slept in its rime:
the order of words does not distract the world.

There is a place where the shepherd's flute dares its transparency
(mud has made hair into chamfron, depolished breath)
 nothing is raised up on the sacred flagstones, save what is admitted to veneration
 poets and storytellers deliberately obliterate the page or silence acclamation,
 triumph has withheld its maw from us, glaucous eternity for me.

Palm-tree faces, pumped up with blood, which hoists the canopy with wind
 the town raises its rampart which offers up salutation to us
 a man acknowledges losing his teeth, rotting in sand, like time, a woman
 goes to sleep on the river then rises, pregnant-with-supplication! . . .

Hear this place, where lust arms its vessel, meanness rises into thistles.
 The aborted laugh of the dead man has imprinted the cheek of the living
 faceless slaver wanders in the depths of the desert, where mirages strive,
 every poem changes and space has hardened its winnower.

It is nothing to oppose so many fields of thorns
To oppose these ensconced poets, magi without diadems,
To oppose the wind that bites in the insult,
To oppose what is sliced into itches
with dumb silence unstrung from the husk.

Oh this time the eye has found its lid.

The fable-born beast has composed
cloud, which pushes into river, dies
in the east from its redoubling.

It raises two panels which are so many arcs of filaos,
two churchyards of infinity where more than one port will have
soured, and then
the scarab, at heavy noon, which exhorts itself to shine
in its Ray! . . . Dumb with the same dubbing.

The yellow wind has growled over sand, the fire collapses:
"Your soul
becomes sun! . . ." The fire
collapses into desecrated rushes. A man acknowledges

pushing into night, body after death, on this mangrove where he writes,
until the heart's swerving, like a felled wasp,
when the red flower blooms behind fatigue,
—the grass stumbles in this brilliance.

He says these arboreal misconducts called out to him
the ones sown—naked—in the outpost of sands,
their voices spell in sulfured bits: "I weave
the truth into your sunlight . . ." The offended tree
then avows swamps, so many islets that make a braying sound, a branch
which evaporates in crazed fire and trembles.

Oh for this once, the eye has reasoned out its space

the body of earth in fever has broken its rhythm, it has hailed its
hands in blessed unity, it dishevels every star it has taken fault for
thought gives volcano for flower and thin smoke of thorns for path . . .

News of the island clutched to forehead,
shipwrecks of sun and red bouquets of lava,
there we tie our words, so weak and easy to unravel,
—exhausted words, running the river to divert our harbors . . .

Whoever loves is wild grass in vagrancy.
In roads known and unknown he has staked the same lineage
offer him some of this millet that was bartered from eternity
storyteller, he has budded, lay him down at the river that slow
summons,
a prophet's laugh is hard on the clay of this world.

At the uprooted well of time water exhorts this countenance,
plows into the sockets,
unlaces the eye and ravishes it, opens the ages and mixes them, mixes
the maimed with the salted wind purveyor of blood, enumerates in a
dahlia so many tortures consented to, raises on the pulley of rocks an
entire past of numb filth
(arms in the poet a plunderer of herds)
and flows between the desolate sands.

Then I took up this rock and made it ring.

The light of words settled naked on the peace of the grass
the morning left a fire of wind-forlorn leaves in the cabin
the barred daylight came down the mountain
touduvan, marchatouffle, dreamtreacle, melanesia
all words of dying and noon
barkers of blood.

"My beloved body, see the straits to which summer has delivered us
in this cold which, level with the sun, so haunts us!"—The wind
to the blue moon recounts a pretty-passage.

This meadow lies down in a jungle, a well forces destruction
the news-in-Creole has at last roughcast its Nile . . .

Sillac and acoma ring out new laghia
sillac, the wake of the animal in its Advent
acoma, old brush raised into a single shaft
laghia, youthful fray beniled by an eternity . . .

The blaze, born of red barley, much praised for modesty
advances, prizing Gorea where our paths laid their braids
He assembles, old body raised into the blueness of time, words of
water and words of rice
   the tree perfumes, the hibiscus, smelling of anise, thrusts out a bee-
eater of tender ovasions . . .

These words you haul out all in a row—which ones do they seem to be?
A combat of dance does not affect advancing seed . . .

Undergrowths of stones converge here at the acacia-temples down
below, the keeper of the Plantation lives in a skinny reed
   its verdure has become a swelling mass of guano,
   the news of the bank will have fallen by the depths, O Transparent
Ones.

A reddish perfume tastes the rough silence,
ten camel-drivers run down the track, cheering the animals
the water of all-sand is a forgotten island . . .

In the flank of the burning sluice, someone inspired has given up
more than linen and veils: Laoka O Laoka! She offers a little water to the
river, then raises her purified heart to the open wind,
   the shadow of the reeds all around splashes up,

on the ridge a donkey, when oblong, took offense!
   So the storyteller keeps watch in his oath, swearing to Isis that he will
again become her Ichneumon! . . .

The prow of his cry raises over the mud a quantity of violet peaks,
his destiny, which suddenly digs in at the edge of a cloud, alone . . .

They have leased water overflowing with blood
flung a house on every cabin
they cry out—it is their harborage—a water-eagle in the high wind,
so long raving
they squeeze this lot of rivers into canteens:
the words from afar that ooze on their hands—on the filth of the
pier . . .

In the feigning dark the words run aghast
the god's eye found again in the gray style of hypogeums.

Wooded Regions

The river Lézarde has lost all trace of the great rivers, and run away in streamlets beneath the ruins. Leaving only clods of words and debris exposed to view. Just so the poem, when it strains to trace out the landscape, unravels, rough and allusive. It is naturally an island landscape, in which the sea insinuates and is esteemed. When it rains, mantou crabs overrun the airport runways. The word convokes fabulous or extinct animals: Armadillos, raccoons, pillory rats (a native species), the sea-cow, the secretary-bird—to say the going-on of things. Also the riddle of those who went far away from themselves: false sun-worshippers, false deciders, speakers of nothing. Our resource is in the havoc of the land, where no intelligence has decided things. Do not fear obscurities. Every voice is interwoven with water, primordial or sadly polluted. Generator of the poem. The river Lézarde has lost all trace of red water. The builders have dammed it with cement. Clods of words, debris of earth.

This little bit of sand at the edge of loving
Is moved by earth. A child turns
He sees peoples naked with night
Expanses of sea toward which hatred gyres
Cities staked on fake noise
Water heaved back wind capsized
Always fleeing far away from him.

The beyond descends into this iguana, contempt there.

We have not run in the wind
Nor in the cliff-gorges painted high up our old rains.
We pass away for a thousand years in the quarters of the water.

Far from crystal, screw-nut
Far from the night in which the animal fills the pond
Armadillos, raccoons, and the silent Stars

In that place which is not named, where with sails lowered lies
    What Escaped.

Wharf rat chased pillory rat, going back a long time.

To mud from mud but keeping the mud high.
For one word of the past that does not go against the stream.

The fabulous melopoiea (the stars! the stars!) of smoke without support
    or sides
Far from us the scholar who neither raves nor lashes out,
Very far from us, who pretends to function and commentary.

Branches. Vagabond root.

Sea-cow, where to see sulphur at noon
Secretary-snake that devotes a message to depths
Dreamt glaucous, in a dance so forgotten
Of chains and balls—nailed into the sea.

This sun lies, this sun lies! It falls in freshets
From working its death so brief, there to dig
A blue bit of coal, rendered musty by fires.
The sun, even limited, and we.

There we live, hunger dying
There we perish, crazy hand
Buried in the fold made
By rays of night placed in orbits,
Voice after voice enumerated
We exhaust the lime.

From wind dreamt by land that land has plowed may the meaning imputed depart

Not clear, gentle meaning in which time to bind time, no more than land where unluckily are heard

No more intruders from the sea, let there proceed only land in which salt water has streaked its fire,

But this land worse than a vow, which spreads out in its dust . . .

Dreamt and summoned, where neither thirst nor the thirsty make fun

Idea of land that little wind shall have furnished, crop rotation

Named to abandon beauty which is born to misfortune

In this havoc where all night is scattered

And on your leash to go shall have vaunted its share.

All rivers die at their abyss,
There weir is rigged, poison foams
So dies the Lézarde in its enclosure.

Yet in the defunct vertigo of ebony trees
There is not one hand that does not tremble with the drowned past.

Pale from imploring the clay in which the Reignant serve, they
Start, turn white as chalk upon their eyelet.
Resolve. Distribute. Cut up the land gone.
Hail that in their hand this fist shriveled.
That no Other will come there again.

I speak not for you nor for our eyes without face or memory nor
To uncrown living sap
But for todays running after tomorrow
With so many pasts aflame.

This cry, more severe than a knot of aloes on a slope.

The ochre of earth has not coiled, its speech has not burned time.

They tear out some words that fall, ash and must in their mouths.

They plunder the thing that cries out from their sleep, which they call winnower.

They do not see this Circumlocution pour from them, faraway banyan trees.

Water carts water which flows into water
In it he wears out the year of words
In proportion to your gallops
While an entire people is there, *naked*
Wellspring taking hold in green depths
We who have all chairs, seen
And shout after the departed child.

The Volcano's Water

for Apocal

This large stream and river are in the depths. They roll and rummage, from buried lavas to exposed salt marshes. From the volcano's entrail, in the north of the country of Martinique, to the sands of the south, by paths buried in mangroves and bays. Descent into knowledge. Subterranean geography, which gives force to the world's expanse. Do not fear the depths. There we see pass before us characters of unfathomable myth, Ata-Eli, the Enofis, who keep their secret. The vagrant follows a cloud, by traces and depths, held up by the wind, without respite. They say he is insane . . . When the traveler awakes from such a river, lava comes as sand to the tideless beaches. The word emerges, all the way in the south of the imaginary. It unfurls and guides.

A fault line, heaved up from a stone . . .

The poet goes down, without guide or tackle, without bank or sextant or outcry remaining
And the imprint of the volcano opens him with a water of sand.

He went down, the running fire froze inside him, without silk-winders or pain
This accumulation of lavas in his midst was kindness
A tree, a tree that believes itself, clambered up in that flow
And foretold to the wind a mass of stones burning.

And the markets of colonial rhymes, of tasteless arum, white pepper, and the expectorations from which nothingness grew large for us, also hope, hope obstinate as a breadfruit pudding,
Everything with it incubated, fell into Pelée.

He went far down the White River, and saw that it was red.
It was red as a windless dream.

The trace took hold in the Mount's crater. Not a single rock loosened.
The cloud, the very cloud, becoming a vow, stole away the fetter
Camellias came there, flowerings of Balata
He walked on the underside of earth, heel forward
As the story says: He invented noon before the singing morn.

He fell into the other side of his own truth, across a bridge, and the
bridge
In flames, ran into the abyss
From careless height to itinerant lowland.

The other side of truth said to him: "This river sounded white when
it joined the Lézarde
At Junction, where a long-beast made a triangle with the water of the
bamboos."
It said: "This is true. I have seen its triangular soul at the prow. It
went far away from us, carefully.
Tracing its aim in the wrinkled water."

In the water he breathed semblance of the Black Beloved
For simulation may provide access to reality
Not so if this were land or sweet melancholy
Or a delicate rock on the fire?

"I have named you, of a new domain of action, time of cane syrup
and scuffle
Flame up from the boat in which we have so long ripened, I have
named you
Passage, in which I took from the wind its palm, from memory
its like
From water its taste for the prow and I have sealed your simulacrum
and I
In the odor of your pale name, Ata-Eli, have disassembled
The bank that does not proceed, the water that does not bear, in
which you would name me."

Or what if, in this clamor of flames, fires, and furies,
It were flames that laughed at their perpetual semblance in him?

In the same mirror was stowed this prophecy
Guys derived from the loftiest past.

They who assembled a crowd of brats far from the hut, they
barricaded the silence
　With a fire of cooked leaves, as would be done to contused people,
then raised a boiler of water
　In the middle of the hut, and recited over the water
　Betrampled maledictions, a cloth bound their heads, the children
　Thought it was fever, pain, and cataplasm, it was
　To cite the truth toward the depths, pain without memory . . .

By the same memory was stowed cry
Of prophetic tale and telling wind.

He went down. A pure executioner dipped into the thread of water
his hachet, his chisel
　And bound land in Mali to the divided Ande.
　He greets him. Torches of moon, rags of lava, pierce the ploughshare.
Cities
　Rise up, filaos candelabra'd with fire. Thousands
　Of nameless gods search for the poem's planted field.

A haul of the Righteous held the bridge. They said: "We wouldn't
know, in so much obscurity. Which wind is this? Where, this rush?
What, this opacity?"

He left them. He went down.
A Shadow there had been frightened for a long time.

—"What my Columbus," he said, "yet again you bestir your
madness, yet again?
We know that you come back every five hundred fifty-five years
By tide of the depths which is emitted from volcano to beach,
Thicker than ashes of stone that turn to salt
You are more eternal than unlashed suffering, this we know."

—"O Stupefied One. My tormented eyes have thrown me
Toward where infinity suffers neither measure nor dial,
No more no farther, neither for the steeped Indian nor for the Child-
King
Whose hand is held up when he seals the Statutes.

I dimly recollect having never armed the heavy crawling fish
Nor lain waste to their den with a boatful of overripe Africans
Hardly had I beaten so many thousands of Arawaks
When it became necessary. O Stupefied One, see
The dead of the past, what do they weigh upon yesterday's dead?
What can compass and map do for machines that see at night
Shouting at the hand with a finger that presses the button?
And so trembled I with uplifting fire
Is it the same truth?"

Well, neglecting answer, and restoring vigil
For a long time he retained a penitent driver
From among those who take from cloud compass map and heavy
sextants.

He came to a Plateau
Whence extended neither lowland nor height.

He ransacked Mountain and dead sands. And under the sand, the do-
nothing dead
And words twisted by the lack of meaning. He engrafted the words
In an auction of thirteen languages interweaving
In wounded Unity.

Death is of a unity
Where are wounded
Only vain retrieved sands.

The rising echo cried out: "Do not trample the exclamation. Be done
with the surge." The echo declined, ah! unhauled its double, which cried
out thus.
　"There are words that burn where they are, they are only good once.
　They appear not to craft nor to beauty of usage,
　And there is no language in a country where all languages are
astonished
　The order of words distracts the world . . ."

He went down into the surge of woods.

In the surging tide the Vigils rise up.

Those who make windy music which is naked and exposed.
Those that still joust at Joux. Those who name the nights of a hut in
the Elysée. All those who go forth with painted, uprooted hair. Tasters
of thin sausage or vacillating fat. Those ballasted with balls for the green
depths. Those whose hams smoke and wink. Giddy females who care
nothing for red dye. Who eat dirt and lead this army.

He undertakes the hard strophe where is praised
Neither fullness of verse nor sweetness of the acclaimed
But winds stream there, surges fell.
Rigidity of hands and naked acclamations.

The fire swelled in Lamentin, where a girl felt with her foot beneath
the mangrove.
　At once she knew the volcano's water, in the frozen water of the bay.
　A fleshy drum thrashed the blood, making salinities of years rise up,
　Calling from hot to cold and cold to a vow that is strangled.
　An initiated girl. ——

They said to him: "We acquit you of night. Of wind. Of obscurity.
We grant your worthiness, from depths to expanse.
May the outline proceed through our bodies, belaved corpses
From Pelée to Cohée to Diamant unoccupied . . ."

Then he made a sign to me to walk in the land. But still a child, I could not
Follow the Enofis who followed him in the water of fire.

Famines of water! And raucous blindnesses of those athirst.
They say: "It is the land, the bitched land, the thoroughly exhausted land
Which melds its swell to the water's disorder."

This mango has cried out its faded fire on the planks of the tray.

Miscreants sulfured by the typhoons you thunder
Children drained into so many mornings
A woman walking with a dead baby goat at her breast.

He sees how, in all this cry, a slow country of sand soughed and rattled, and how this boat navigated on our fugitive anguishes
And how we hail in our hands a little of that rain, from which talented mud, and white felony occurred among us and how
O sandmen, the growth of your Pelées burned us.

Lavas. Sap of fire, slow water.

And there rose up the One missing from the sand, who hastens toward the way of the All-world.
"What are you up to down there, O denizen of the Lower-World?"
The water of the Canal gaped toward the orchards of Lebanon.
And the lair of the Mountain rolled a hut in Anse.
"Go great prose of their cry, that resonated through Pointe-à-Pitre.
Incite singing in the Islands, rain upon the lost, blue patience! And all exposed dregs."

And all exposed life, in the old cyclone of the year! . . . He goes up in the sea, he is pious . . . He has tied a pitiful scarf around the throat of the mountain . . . And this idea that proceeds, thundering venom and yellow current . . . Like a sowing of *chadron!* . . . Like milk from a mad *bécune!* . . . All the way to raising the bucket of water, nacreous with a heaviness of words, up where the stone plays with the red of corn, all belongs to the eve of the Trace.

Fault lines, that rise up.

NOTES

Balata: A place in Martinique.
Pelées: A volcanic mountain in the northern part of the island of Martinique.

Note

Bécune, chadron, mantou, and vonvon are species of Antillean fauna.

The bel-air is a very precise dance, which traces figures upon the dance floor.

Bézaudin is a mountain in Martinique, known for the quality of its storytellers and its drummers.

Cayali, flambant, frigate, messenger, ortolan, pipiri, sugar-bird: these are birds that have disappeared from our landscapes.

Laghia. Creolists recommend the spelling Ladja, but this to my mind caresses too sweetly.

Mabi is a drink, migan is something to eat, manjé-kouli is "eating by a coolie."

Knowledge in a genuine abyss.

NOTE

laghia: See note on laghia in "Fastes."

Édouard Glissant (1928–2011) was one of the most influential postcolonial theorists, novelists, playwrights, and poets—not only in the Caribbean but also in contemporary French letters. He was a finalist for the Nobel Prize in Literature twice and the recipient of the Prix Renaudot and the Prix Charles Veillon in France. His works include *Poetics of Relation*; *Caribbean Discourse*; *Faulkner, Mississippi*; and the novel *The Ripening*. He was Distinguished Professor of French at Graduate Center, City University of New York.

Jeff Humphries was Louisiana State University Foundation Distinguished Professor of French, English, and Comparative Literature. He published several books of poetry, fiction, essays, and literary criticism, including *Borealis* (Minnesota, 2002).

Melissa Manolas studied comparative literature at Louisiana State University. She has also translated work by Josée Lapeyrère.